EDITOR: Maryanne Blacker
FOOD EDITOR: Pamela Clark

• • •

ASSISTANT FOOD EDITOR: Jan Castorina
ART DIRECTOR: Robbylee Phelan
SUB-EDITOR: Bridget van Tinteren
EDITORIAL CO-ORDINATOR: Fiona Nicholas

• • •

PHOTOGRAPHERS: Ben Eriksson,
Rodney Weidland, Andre Wohler

• • •

ACP PUBLISHER: Richard Walsh
ACP DEPUTY PUBLISHER: Nick Chan

• • •

Produced by The Australian Women's Weekly
Home Library
Typeset by ACP Colour Graphics Pty Ltd.
Printed by Times Printers Pte Ltd, Singapore.
Published by ACP Publishing, 54 Park Street Sydney

• • •

♦ **USA:** Distributed for Whitecap Books Ltd by Graphic Arts
Center Publishing, 3019 N.W. Yeon, Portland, OR, 97210.
tel: 503-226-2402. Fax: 530-223-1410.

• • •

♦ **CANADA:** Distributed in Canada by Whitecap
Books Ltd, 1086 West 3rd St, North Vancouver, B.C.
V7P 3J6. Tel: 604- 980-9852. Fax: 604-980-8097

• • •

• • •

FRONT COVER: Sweet and Sour Pork, page 42.
Watermelon in Ginger Wine, page 96.
BACK COVER: Chicken and Corn Soup, page 16. Butterfly
Shrimp, page 36. Fried Rice, page 90. Lychees and
Mandarin Ice, page 100.
OPPOSITE: Crab in Gingerroot Sauce, page 38.

CHINESE
COOKING CLASS COOKBOOK

You can quickly learn to cook a fabulous feast of Chinese food with our easy step-by-step recipes selected by former Food Editor Ellen Sinclair. We show you how to create the subtle tastes and textures of your favorite dishes, plus restaurant specials and other clever but deliciously simple recipes. There are tips, too, for an essential accompaniment – perfect steamed rice. Fried rice, more substantial, could be eaten as a meal on its own. Although there aren't many desserts in this cuisine, we've included a few traditional ones and lots of lovely extras.

Pamela Clark
FOOD EDITOR

FOR YOUR INFORMATION: Most of the special ingredients used in Chinese cooking are now available at large supermarkets and food stores. You may have to visit Chinese food stores to buy specialized items. The number of servings given in each recipe takes into account the fact that in a Chinese meal three or four dishes might be served at once.

HORS D'OEUVRE

A plate of two or three different hors d'oeuvre make a deliciously light start to a Chinese meal.

Stuffed Mushrooms

YOU WILL NEED
20 medium-sized mushrooms
all-purpose flour
oil for deep-frying

STUFFING
½lb ground pork
4 green onions, chopped
½ red bell pepper, finely chopped
1 stalk celery, finely chopped
¼ cup finely chopped water chestnuts
1 tablespoon grated fresh gingerroot
4 teaspoons dry sherry
2 teaspoons light soy sauce
1 teaspoon hoisin sauce
1 egg white
2 teaspoons cornstarch

BATTER
⅓ cup cornstarch
⅓ cup all-purpose flour
1 teaspoon double-acting baking powder
¼ cup water
¼ cup milk

1. Remove stems from mushrooms. Finely chop stems, reserve for stuffing. Fill cavities of mushrooms with stuffing, mounding in center as shown.

2. Coat mushrooms with flour, dip in prepared batter. Deep-fry mushrooms, 4 at a time, in hot oil until golden brown and cooked through, approximately 5 minutes; drain on absorbent paper. Do not have oil too hot or mushrooms will brown too quickly and not cook through.

Stuffing: Combine all ingredients with reserved mushroom stems in bowl; mix well.

Batter: Sift dry ingredients into bowl, make well in center, gradually add milk and water; mix to a smooth batter.
Makes 20.

Note: Recipe can be prepared several hours ahead. Batter and deep-fry mushrooms just before serving.

Egg Rolls

YOU WILL NEED
3 tablespoons cornstarch
½ cup water
25 egg roll skins
oil for deep-frying

FILLING
1lb large uncooked
**   shrimp, shelled**
8oz can water chestnuts
1in piece fresh gingerroot
1lb ground pork
8 green onions, chopped
1 red bell pepper,
**   finely chopped**
¼lb mushrooms, sliced
½ Chinese cabbage,
**   finely shredded**
¼ cup dry sherry
4 teaspoons light
**   soy sauce**
1 teaspoon sugar
4 teaspoons vegetable oil

Note: Egg roll skins are available from Asian food stores. Egg rolls can be prepared several hours ahead. Deep-fry just before serving.

1. Combine cornstarch and water in bowl. Spoon a tablespoon of filling evenly across one corner of each egg roll skin, fold in sides, roll up in an envelope shape, brushing edges with cornstarch mixture. Deep-fry egg rolls in batches in hot oil until golden brown and cooked through; drain on absorbent paper.

2. **Filling:** Devein and chop shrimp; chop water chestnuts. Grate gingerroot finely.

3. Combine shrimp, water chestnuts, gingerroot, pork, onions, pepper, mushrooms, cabbage, sherry, sauce and sugar in bowl; mix well. Heat oil in pan, add pork mixture, cook, stirring, 4 minutes. Remove from pan; cool.
Makes 25.

Ham Balls

YOU WILL NEED
2 large boneless, skinless
**   chicken breast halves**
½lb leg ham
8oz can bamboo shoots,
**   drained**
8oz can water chestnuts,
**   drained**
1oz Chinese dried
**   mushrooms**
¼ cup vegetable oil
3 tablespoons dry sherry
1 tablespoon soy sauce
½ teaspoon Oriental
**   sesame oil**
4 teaspoons cornstarch
extra cornstarch
oil for deep-frying

BATTER
½ cup cornstarch
½ cup all-purpose flour
1 teaspoon double-acting
**   baking powder**
¾ cup cold water
1 egg white

1. Chop chicken, ham, bamboo shoots and water chestnuts finely. Cover mushrooms with hot water in bowl, stand 30 minutes; drain. Remove stems, chop mushrooms finely.

Note: It is important to roll the balls gently; if rolled too firmly they will crumble slightly. Mixture can be made a day ahead. Make batter just before using. Batter and deep-fry ham balls just before serving.

2. Heat oil in wok or skillet, add all chopped ingredients, stir-fry 3 minutes. Add combined sherry and sauce, sesame oil and cornstarch, cook 2 minutes; cool.

3. Gently roll tablespoons of mixture into balls; coat balls lightly with cornstarch.

4. Place 4 balls into batter. Gently lift balls from batter, draining slightly. Deep-fry balls in hot oil until browned; drain on absorbent paper. Repeat with remaining balls.

Batter: Sift dry ingredients into bowl, gradually stir in water until smooth. Just before using, beat egg-white in small bowl until soft peaks form; fold into batter.
Makes about 45.

Gow Gees

YOU WILL NEED
45 wonton skins
2oz Chinese dried
 mushrooms
¼lb uncooked shrimp
½ cup bamboo shoots
½lb ground pork
6 green onions, finely
 chopped
1 teaspoon grated
 fresh gingerroot
1 clove garlic, minced
2 teaspoons Oriental
 sesame oil
4 teaspoons light
 soy sauce
4 teaspoons dry sherry
oil for deep-frying
SWEET AND SOUR SAUCE
½ cup sugar
¾ cup water
½ cup white vinegar
3 tablespoons tomato
 paste
4 teaspoons tomato
 ketchup
4 teaspoons cornstarch
¼ cup water, extra

1. Using a cutter, cut wonton skins into 3 inch rounds. You can stack and cut several skins together.

2. Cover mushrooms with hot water in bowl, stand 30 minutes; drain. Remove stems; finely chop mushrooms. Shell and finely chop shrimp. Finely chop bamboo shoots. Combine mushrooms, shrimp and bamboo shoots with pork, onions, gingerroot, garlic, sesame oil, sauce and sherry; mix well.

3. Spoon mixture into center of each round. Brush edges of rounds with water, fold in half, pinch edges together firmly.

4. Deep-fry gow gees in batches in hot oil until golden brown; drain on absorbent paper. Serve with sauce.

Sweet and Sour Sauce: Combine sugar, water, vinegar, paste and ketchup in pan, stir over heat until sugar is dissolved. Stir in blended cornstarch and extra water, stir until sauce boils and thickens, simmer 1 minute.
Makes 45.

Note: Recipe can be prepared several hours ahead. Deep-fry just before serving.

Chicken and Banana Squares

YOU WILL NEED
6 slices white bread
4 boneless, skinless
 chicken breast halves
2 firm bananas
2 eggs, lightly beaten
¼ cup milk
all-purpose flour
2 cups fresh bread crumbs
oil for deep-frying

1. Remove crusts from bread, cut each slice into 4 squares. Steam or poach chicken until tender; cool. Cut each piece of chicken in half horizontally to make 8 thin slices; cut each slice into 3. Peel bananas, cut in half horizontally. Cut each length of banana into pieces the same size as the chicken.

2. Brush one side of each piece of bread with combined eggs and milk. Place a piece of chicken on top of the egg-glazed side, place a piece of banana on top of the chicken.

3. Holding chicken and banana firmly onto the bread, coat chicken and banana squares lightly with flour. Dip in egg mixture, coat well with bread crumbs. Repeat once more with egg mixture and bread crumbs.

4. Deep-fry squares in batches in hot oil until golden brown; drain on absorbent paper.
Makes 24.

Note: Recipe can be prepared several hours ahead. Assemble, crumb and deep-fry squares just before serving.

Ham and Chicken Rolls

YOU WILL NEED
2 whole chicken breasts
¼ teaspoon pepper
¼ teaspoon five-spice
powder
1 clove garlic, minced
4 slices cooked ham
4 egg roll skins
all-purpose flour
1 egg, lightly beaten
3 tablespoons milk
oil for deep-frying

Note: Do not have oil too hot or rolls will brown too quickly and not cook through. Recipe can be prepared a day ahead. Deep-fry rolls just before serving.

1. Remove skin from chicken breasts. Using sharp knife, carefully remove chicken meat from bones to make 4 pieces. Separate the fillet which runs along the bone on either side.

2. Pound breast pieces and fillet pieces out separately until very thin, taking care not to tear meat. Lay fillet piece on top of each breast piece, pound lightly. Spread chicken pieces with combined pepper, five-spice powder and garlic. Roll each slice of ham and place on top of chicken, roll up firmly. Fold in ends.

3. Toss chicken rolls in flour, then dip in combined egg and milk. Place a chicken roll diagonally across each egg roll skin. Fold in ends and roll up securely. Seal ends with a little egg mixture.

4. Deep-fry rolls in hot oil until golden brown and cooked through; drain on absorbent paper. Cut rolls into diagonal slices, serve with sweet and sour sauce (see recipe on page 6).

Pork Wontons

YOU WILL NEED
½lb uncooked shrimp,
shelled
1lb ground pork
¼ Chinese cabbage,
finely shredded
6 green onions,
finely chopped
1 egg
3 tablespoons cornstarch
2 teaspoons light
soy sauce
2 teaspoons Oriental
sesame oil
50 wonton skins
oil for deep-frying

Note: Recipe can be prepared several hours ahead. Deep-fry just before serving.

1. Devein shrimp, chop 8 shrimp; reserve. Chop remaining shrimp finely. Combine finely chopped shrimp, pork, cabbage, onions, egg, cornstarch, sauce and sesame oil in bowl; mix well. Place a teaspoon of mixture onto center of each wonton skin.

2. Gather the sides of skins around filling, pleating edges.

4. Deep-fry wontons in batches in hot oil until golden brown; drain on absorbent paper. Makes 50.

3. Place a piece of reserved shrimp on top of each wonton.

Hors d'oeuvre Rolls

YOU WILL NEED
¾lb piece frozen puff
   pastry, thawed
1 egg, lightly beaten
oil for deep-frying

FILLING
½ cup roughly broken
   fine egg noodles
2 tablespoons (¼ stick)
   butter
¼lb ground pork
2oz mushrooms,
   finely chopped
6 green onions,
   finely chopped
½lb cooked shrimp,
   shelled, deveined
1 hard-boiled egg,
   finely chopped
4 teaspoons dry sherry

*Note: Recipe can be prepared
a day ahead. Deep-fry just
before serving.*

1. Cut pastry in half, roll each half into a 13 inch x 16 inch rectangle. Using a sharp knife, trim pastry to a 12 inch x 15 inch rectangle. Cut each piece into 5 x 3 inch strips, then each strip into 4 x 3 inch squares.

2. Place a heaped teaspoon of mixture along center of each square, leaving edges free. Glaze edges with egg.

3. Roll up pastry tightly, pressing edges together to seal. Deep-fry rolls in batches in hot oil until golden brown; drain on absorbent paper. Serve with sweet and sour sauce (see recipe on page 6).

4. **Filling:** Cook noodles in boiling salted water about 3 minutes or until tender, rinse under hot water; drain. Finely chop noodles. Heat butter in skillet, add pork, stir until well browned. Add mushrooms and onions, cook, stirring, further 2 minutes. Remove from heat, add noodles, finely chopped shrimp, egg and sherry; mix well.
Makes 40.

Pork and Lettuce Rolls

YOU WILL NEED
2oz Chinese dried
   mushrooms
6 green onions,
   finely chopped
4 teaspoons vegetable oil
½lb ground pork
½ x 8oz can water
   chestnuts, drained,
   finely chopped
½ cup bamboo shoots,
   finely chopped
6oz can crabmeat
2 teaspoons Oriental
   sesame oil
4 teaspoons light
   soy sauce
2 teaspoons oyster-
   flavored sauce
3 tablespoons dry sherry
8 lettuce leaves

*Note: Recipe can be prepared
several hours ahead. Stir-fry to
reheat just before serving.*

1. Cover mushrooms with hot water in bowl, stand 30 minutes; drain. Remove stems, finely chop mushrooms. Finely chop onions.

2. Heat vegetable oil in wok or skillet, add pork, stir-fry until golden brown. Add mushrooms, onions, water chestnuts, bamboo shoots and crabmeat, stir-fry 1 minute. Add combined sesame oil, sauces and sherry to wok, stir-fry until combined; remove from heat.

3. Divide pork mixture evenly between lettuce leaves.

4. Fold in ends and sides of lettuce leaves as shown, roll up to form a neat package. Generally the pork filling and lettuce leaves are served separately; guests fill and roll their own lettuce leaves.
Makes 8 rolls.

SOUPS

Chinese soups come in two varieties: light and clear, thick and hearty. Our favorites are featured in this section.

Mongolian Hot Pot

Mongolian Hot Pot, Chinese Steamboat – the dish of many names –is a fun way of cooking for a small party. The cooking vessel can be purchased in Asian food stores, or use a fondue set instead. Heat the chicken broth before pouring it into the fondue pot.

The pot is set in the center of the table, guests add their own choice of food to the simmering broth. Small strainers, shown in picture, are for lifting the food from the broth into individual small bowls.

When all the food has been eaten, the broth forms the last course of the meal.

Accompaniments set around the pot could include: soy sauce, chili sauce, hoisin sauce, Oriental sesame oil, barbeque sauce or lemon sauce (all available from most large supermarkets or Asian food stores). Grated fresh gingerroot mixed with a little sugar and dry white wine, is a good accompaniment. Also have a large bowl of steamed rice.

TO PREPARE THE POT
Use heat beads available for use in barbeques. The beads must be set alight, then burnt until they are white hot; the best way to do this is in a barbeque or hibachi.

While the heat beads are burning, stand the hot pot on a very thick piece of solid wood to protect the surface on which the pot stands. Using tongs, quickly place the white hot beads down the pot's chimney, then pour the boiling stock into the pot.

An electric hot pot (which simplifies the preparation) or a large electric skillet can be used.

YOU WILL NEED
8oz piece beef tenderloin
2 pork tenderloins
4 boneless, skinless chicken breast halves
2 large fish fillets
1lb uncooked jumbo shrimp
¼lb bean sprouts
¼lb snow peas
8oz can bamboo shoots, drained, thinly sliced
1 carrot, thinly sliced
15oz can baby corn, drained
24 shucked oysters or one large bottle oysters
½ Chinese cabbage, coarsely shredded
¼lb bean curd, cubed
15oz can straw mushrooms, drained, halved
6oz rice vermicelli
CHICKEN BROTH
3 chicken backs (or other chicken pieces)
10 cups water
3 chicken bouillon cubes
1 stalk celery, chopped
2in piece fresh gingerroot, sliced
1 medium onion, sliced
½ teaspoon Oriental sesame oil
4 green onions, chopped

1. Remove all fat and sinew from beef and pork, wrap in plastic wrap, place in freezer 1 hour or until very firm. With very sharp knife or cleaver, cut beef and pork into ⅛ inch slices. Cut chicken into thin slices. Remove skin and bones from fish. Cut fish into 2 inch x ¼ inch slices. Shell and devein shrimp; if large, cut lengthways into 2. Wash bean sprouts, top and tail snow peas.

2. Arrange all ingredients on platters, place around prepared hot pot with bowls of accompaniments.

Chicken Broth: Combine chicken backs, water, crumbled bouillon cubes, celery, gingerroot and sliced onion in pan. Simmer, covered, 2 hours, strain broth, return broth to pan, add sesame oil and green onions, bring to boil, remove from heat. To serve, bring broth to boil then pour into hot pot.
Serves 6 to 8.

Note: Recipe can be prepared several hours ahead. Boil stock and prepare pot just before serving.

Crab Combination Soup

YOU WILL NEED

1oz Chinese dried mushrooms
¼lb sea scallops
6oz can crabmeat
8 green onions, chopped
½ x 8oz can bamboo shoots
1 egg
1 teaspoon vegetable oil
6 cups chicken broth
½ teaspoon grated fresh gingerroot
2 chicken bouillon cubes, crumbled
4 teaspoons light soy sauce
4 teaspoons dry sherry
¼ cup cornstarch
¼ cup water
2 egg whites
3 tablespoons water, extra

Note: Recipe can be prepared several hours ahead. Cook just before serving.

1. Cover mushrooms with hot water in bowl, stand 30 minutes; drain. Remove stems, slice mushrooms thinly. Wash scallops. Using sharp knife, remove dark vein, slice scallops thinly. Drain and flake crabmeat. Chop onions. Cut bamboo shoots into strips.

2. Lightly beat egg with fork. Heat oil in small skillet, add egg, swirl egg to coat side and base of skillet evenly. Loosen edges of omelet with spatula, turn and cook other side. Remove from skillet, roll up, cut into thin strips.

3. Boil chicken broth in large pan, add mushrooms, scallops, crabmeat, onions, bamboo shoots and gingerroot, bring to boil, simmer 2 minutes. Stir in combined bouillon cubes, sauce, sherry and blended cornstarch and water. Stir until boiling, simmer, uncovered, 2 minutes.

4. Beat egg whites and extra water lightly, add to soup in a thin stream; stir well.
Serves 6.

Long Soup

YOU WILL NEED

¼ small cabbage
8 green onions
½lb lean pork
4 teaspoons vegetable oil
6 cups chicken broth
2 chicken bouillon cubes
2 tablespoons light soy sauce
½ teaspoon grated fresh gingerroot
¼lb fine egg noodles
3 green onions, sliced, extra

Note: Recipe can be prepared several hours ahead. Cook just before serving.

1. Finely shred cabbage. Cut onions into thin diagonal slices. Slice pork into shreds.

2. Heat oil in wok or skillet, add shredded pork and cabbage, stir-fry 3 minutes.

3. Add broth, crumbled bouillon cubes, sauce and gingerroot. Bring slowly to boil, reduce heat, add onions, simmer 10 minutes.

4. Meanwhile, add noodles to pan of boiling water, boil until just tender; drain well. To serve, place noodles in soup bowls, pour hot soup over, sprinkle with extra onions.
Serves 8.

Chicken and Corn Soup

YOU WILL NEED
2lb chicken or chicken pieces
8 cups water
4 black peppercorns
1in piece fresh gingerroot, sliced
1 onion, quartered
3 sprigs parsley
2 cups canned creamed corn
2 chicken bouillon cubes
½ teaspoon grated fresh gingerroot, extra
5 green onions, chopped
1 teaspoon Oriental sesame oil
⅓ cup cornstarch
⅓ cup water
2 egg whites
3 tablespoons water, extra
2 slices cooked ham, thinly sliced
4 green onions, chopped, extra

1. The base of most Chinese soup is a good chicken broth. A whole chicken can be used. Some of the cooked meat, can be shredded and added to the soup and the remainder used for another meal. However, chicken pieces will serve the same purpose. Place chicken into large pan, add water, peppercorns, gingerroot, onion and parsley. Bring to boil over medium heat, skim well to remove any scum; reduce heat, simmer gently, covered, 1½ hours. Remove any scum from top of broth, strain, reserve 6 cups of broth. Remove meat from chicken, shred meat finely (you will need about 1 cup shredded chicken for this soup).

2. Combine reserved chicken broth, corn, crumbled bouillon cubes, extra gingerroot, green onions and sesame oil in large pan, bring to boil. Stir in blended cornstarch and water, stir until soup boils and thickens, simmer 1 minute.

3. Lightly beat egg whites and extra water, add to soup in a thin stream, stirring well.

4. Add ham and shredded chicken to soup, heat gently. Top with extra green onions. Serves 6.

Note: *Broth can be made several days ahead or can be frozen. Make soup just before serving.*

Short Soup

YOU WILL NEED
1lb ground pork
¼ small cabbage, shredded
4 teaspoons light soy sauce
½ teaspoon Oriental sesame oil
1 teaspoon grated fresh gingerroot
24 wonton skins
1 egg, lightly beaten
SOUP
8 cups chicken broth
3 green onions, finely chopped
½ teaspoon Oriental sesame oil
1 chicken bouillon cube

Note: *Recipe can be prepared several hours ahead. Cook wontons and add soup just before serving. Uncooked wontons suitable to freeze.*

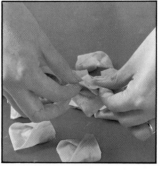

1. Combine pork, cabbage, sauce, sesame oil and gingerroot in small bowl; mix well. Place a teaspoon of pork mixture slightly below center of each wonton skin. Brush edges of skins with egg.

2. Fold skins in half diagonally to form triangles. Press edges to seal, pressing out air pockets around pork mixture. Brush corners with egg; pinch corners together to seal.

4. Drop wontons into large pan of boiling water, boil, uncovered, until wontons float to the surface; drain. Place 3 wontons into each soup bowl, pour over hot soup.

Soup: Combine chicken broth, onions, sesame oil and crumbled bouillon cube in large pan, bring to boil, simmer 3 minutes. Serves 8.

Abalone Soup

YOU WILL NEED

FISH BROTH
10 cups water
2 chicken backs
2 stalks celery, chopped
2 large onions, chopped
5in piece fresh gingerroot, sliced
1 large fish head

SOUP
1lb canned abalone
3 tablespoons vegetable oil
1 teaspoon Oriental sesame oil
1/4lb cooked ham, finely sliced
1 red bell pepper, finely sliced
1/4lb mushrooms, finely sliced
2 stalks celery, finely sliced
3 tablespoons light soy sauce
1 teaspoon sugar
1/3 cup cornstarch
1/2 cup water
2oz rice vermicelli noodles

1. **Fish Broth:** Place water, chicken backs, celery, onions and gingerroot into large pan. Bring to boil, cover, simmer gently 1½ hours. Add fish head, cover, simmer further 20 minutes; cool until warm. Pour broth through fine sieve. Skim any fat from surface of broth.

2. **Soup:** Drain abalone. Using a sharp knife, cut into very thin slices. Heat oil in large pan, add sesame oil, ham and vegetables, stir-fry 3 minutes. Add abalone, fish broth, sauce and sugar. Bring mixture to boil, simmer, covered, 10 minutes.

3. Stir in blended cornstarch and water, stir until soup boils, simmer, covered, 5 minutes. Break noodles in half, add to pan, simmer, uncovered, 5 minutes, stirring occasionally. Serves 8 to 10.

Note: Recipe can be prepared several hours ahead. Cook soup just before serving. Broth is suitable to freeze.

Szechuan Soup

YOU WILL NEED
8 Chinese dried mushrooms
1/2lb cooked shrimp
7 cups chicken broth
1/2 cup dry white wine
4 teaspoons light soy sauce
1/2 teaspoon chili sauce
3 tablespoons cornstarch
1/4 cup water
1/4lb cooked ham, finely sliced
6oz lean pork, finely sliced
1oz Chinese pickles, finely sliced
1/2 x 8oz can water chestnuts, drained, sliced
1/2 red bell pepper, finely sliced
2 teaspoons vinegar
1 teaspoon Oriental sesame oil
1 egg
1 tablespoon water, extra
8 green onions
1/2lb bean curd, cubed

1. Cover mushrooms with hot water in bowl, stand 30 minutes. Remove stems, slice mushrooms thinly. Shell and devein shrimp. Combine chicken broth, wine and sauces in large pan, bring to boil, boil, uncovered, 5 minutes. Gradually stir in blended cornstarch and water, stir until soup boils.

3. Stir in mushrooms, ham, pork, pickles, water chestnuts and pepper. Simmer, uncovered, 5 minutes.

4. Stir in vinegar and sesame oil. Lightly beat egg and extra water with a fork. Gradually add to soup, stirring constantly. Add green onions, bean curd and shrimp, simmer 1 minute. Serves 6.

Note: Recipe best made just before serving.

FISH

Seafood – from crab to shrimp to whole fish – is sensational when given a Chinese flavor. Try some of these recipes soon.

Barbequed Shrimp

YOU WILL NEED
1lb uncooked jumbo shrimp
2 teaspoons cornstarch
1 egg white
1 cup vegetable oil
1 large onion, chopped
1 teaspoon curry powder
¼ teaspoon sugar
2 teaspoons sate sauce
¼ cup heavy cream
½ red bell pepper, sliced
lettuce leaves
brandy, warmed (optional)

1. Shell and devein shrimp. Using sharp knife, cut a deep slit along back of each shrimp. Combine cornstarch and egg white in bowl; mix well. Add shrimp; stand 1 hour.

2. Heat oil in wok or skillet, add shrimp, stir-fry until just cooked, remove from wok; drain well.

3. Drain oil from wok, leaving about ¼ cup oil. Add onion, stir-fry 2 minutes. Add curry powder and sugar, stir-fry 1 minute. Add sauce and cream, stir until boiling, simmer 1 minute; add pepper.

4. Line serving dish with lettuce leaves, spoon shrimp over lettuce. If desired, place small metal bowl in center of shrimp. Fill with warmed brandy and set alight. Pick up shrimp with chopsticks, hold over flame to heat and flavor the shrimp.
Serves 2.

Note: *Recipe can be prepared several hours ahead. Stir-fry close to serving.*

Seafood Combination

YOU WILL NEED
½lb sea scallops
½lb squid
½lb uncooked jumbo shrimp
2 large white fish fillets
3 stalks celery
8 green onions
8oz can water chestnuts
8oz can bamboo shoots
⅓ cup vegetable oil
½ cup water
1 chicken bouillon cube
1 teaspoon Oriental sesame oil
2 teaspoons light soy sauce
1 teaspoon cornstarch
2 teaspoons dry sherry

Note: Recipe can be prepared several hours ahead. Stir-fry just before serving.

1. Remove vein from scallops, wash scallops. Hold squid firmly with one hand, hold head and pull gently to remove head and inside of body in 1 piece. Remove bone which will be found at open end of squid; it looks like a piece of plastic. Wash squid, rub off outer skin. Cut squid down center, score shallow diagonal slashes in diamond pattern on inside surface of squid. Shell and devein shrimp. Skin fish, cut fish into large pieces.

2. Slice celery and onions diagonally. Drain water chestnuts, cut in half. Drain bamboo shoots, slice thinly.

3. Heat half the oil in wok or skillet, add prepared vegetables, stir-fry 2 minutes, remove from wok.

4. Heat remaining oil in wok, add scallops, squid, shrimp and fish, stir-fry until just cooked through. Add combined water, crumbled bouillon cube, sesame oil, sauce and blended cornstarch and sherry, stir until mixture boils. Add vegetables, stir until mixture is heated through. Serves 4.

Scallop and Vegetable Combination

YOU WILL NEED
1lb sea scallops
1oz Chinese dried mushrooms
3 stalks celery
½lb green beans
6 green onions
¼ cup vegetable oil
2 onions, quartered
2 teaspoons grated fresh gingerroot
1 clove garlic, minced
1 cup water
2 chicken bouillon cubes
4 teaspoons light soy sauce
4 teaspoons cornstarch
3 tablespoons dry sherry
½ x 15oz can baby corn, drained

Note: Recipe can be prepared several hours ahead. Stir-fry just before serving.

1. Using small sharp knife cut a slit along dark vein of scallops. Lift out dark vein as shown in picture. Wash well, pat dry.

2. Cover mushrooms with boiling water, stand 20 minutes; drain. Remove stems, slice mushrooms thinly. Slice celery, beans and green onions diagonally.

3. Heat oil in wok or skillet, add celery, beans, onions, gingerroot and garlic, stir-fry 2 minutes. Add combined water, crumbled bouillon cubes, sauce and blended cornstarch and sherry, stir until mixture boils and thickens. Add scallops, corn, mushrooms and onions, simmer until scallops are just cooked. Serves 4.

Shrimp Toast

8 uncooked jumbo shrimp
1 egg, lightly beaten
3 tablespoons cornstarch
4 thick slices of bread
1 hard-boiled egg yolk
1 slice cooked ham
1 green onion, finely
chopped
oil for deep-frying

Note: Recipe can be prepared several hours ahead. Assemble and deep-fry toasts just before serving.

1. Shell and devein shrimp, leaving tails intact. Gently flatten shrimp. Combine egg and cornstarch in small bowl, add shrimp. Mix well to coat shrimp completely.

2. Remove crusts from bread, cut slices in half. Place 1 shrimp, cut-side-down on each piece of bread, gently flatten shrimp on bread with palm of hand. Brush with left-over cornstarch mixture (this will help topping adhere).

3. Chop egg yolk and ham into 8 cubes. Push a cube of egg yolk onto shrimp near tail. Place a cube of ham in center of each shrimp. Place ¼ teaspoon onion at bottom of each shrimp; there should be egg, ham, and onion along center of each shrimp.

4. Gently ease toasts, 2 or 3 at a time, into hot oil, deep-fry until bread is golden and shrimp are cooked through; drain on absorbent paper. Makes 8.

Spicy Shrimp

YOU WILL NEED
2lb uncooked jumbo
shrimp
3 medium onions
¼ cup vegetable oil
4 teaspoons water
lettuce leaves
brandy, warmed (optional)
MARINADE
¼ teaspoon five-spice
powder
¼ teaspoon chili powder
3 tablespoons sate sauce
½ teaspoon curry powder
1 teaspoon cornstarch
½ teaspoon sugar
1 teaspoon light soy sauce
4 teaspoons dry sherry

Note: Recipe can be prepared several hours ahead. Stir-fry just before serving.

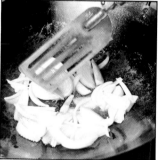

1. Shell and devein shrimp. Using a sharp knife, cut a deep slit along back of shrimp, taking care not to cut right through. Add shrimp to marinade in bowl; mix well. Refrigerate several hours.

2. Cut onions in half, then cut each half into thin wedges. Heat oil in wok or skillet, add onion, stir-fry until transparent.

3. Add shrimp mixture to wok, stir-fry until shrimp are cooked through, add water; mix well. Arrange lettuce leaves on plate, spoon shrimp over lettuce. To serve in the traditional style, place small metal bowl in center of shrimp. Fill with warmed brandy and set alight. Pick up shrimp with chopsticks, hold over flame to heat and flavor shrimp.

Marinade: Combine all ingredients in bowl.
Serves 4.

Crab Claws

YOU WILL NEED
10 thick crab claws
2lb large uncooked shrimp
6 green onions, finely chopped
2 stalks celery, finely chopped
1 tablespoon chopped fresh gingerroot
cornstarch
oil for deep-frying

BATTER
½ cup cornstarch
½ cup all-purpose flour
½ teaspoon double-acting baking powder
1 cup water

SWEET AND SOUR SAUCE
6oz can Chinese mixed pickles
1 teaspoon Chinese chili sauce
1 teaspoon light soy sauce
3 tablespoons tomato ketchup
4 teaspoons sugar
2 teaspoons cornstarch
1 cup water

1. The shell around the fat end of crab claws is generally lightly cracked when purchased. Gently remove the shell from fat end of claw; if necessary, tap gently with mallet or rolling pin to crack the shell further. Do not hit too heavily or crab meat will be damaged. Leave shell on largest nipper, this makes a handle for holding the claw.

2. Shell and devein shrimp. Process shrimp until ground. Combine shrimp with onions, celery and gingerroot in medium bowl; mix well.

3. Divide shrimp mixture evenly into 10 portions. With wet hands, flatten out portions in palm of hand, wrap evenly around crab meat end of crab claws. Coat crab claws lightly with cornstarch.

4. Holding pointed end of crab claws, dip into prepared batter, then deep-fry in hot oil until golden brown and cooked through. Do not have oil too hot or batter will brown too quickly and crab claws will not cook through. Serve one or two crab claws per person with a small bowl of sweet and sour sauce.

Batter: Sift dry ingredients into bowl, make well in center, gradually add water, mix to a smooth batter.

Sweet and Sour Sauce: Drain pickles, place liquid into pan. Shred pickles finely. Place pickles, sauces, ketchup, sugar and blended cornstarch and water into pan with reserved liquid, stir until combined. Stir over heat until sauce boils and thickens, simmer 3 minutes.
Serves 5 or 10.

Note: Recipe can be prepared several hours ahead. Batter and deep-fry just before serving.

Abalone in Oyster Sauce

YOU WILL NEED

1lb canned abalone, drained
1oz Chinese dried mushrooms
6 green onions
1 red bell pepper
1/2 cucumber
1/3 cup vegetable oil
1/2 teaspoon grated fresh gingerroot
3 tablespoons oyster-flavored sauce
2 teaspoons light soy sauce
4 teaspoons white vinegar
1/2 teaspoon sugar
1 chicken bouillon cube
1/2 cup water
1/4 teaspoon Oriental sesame oil
1 tablespoon cornstarch
4 teaspoons dry sherry

Note: Recipe can be prepared several hours ahead. Stir-fry just before serving.

1. Cut abalone into thin slices using a sharp knife.

2. Cover mushrooms with hot water in bowl, stand 30 minutes; drain. Remove stems, slice mushrooms thinly. Cut green onions into diagonal slices. Cut pepper into thin strips. Peel cucumber, cut into quarters lengthways, scoop out seeds; cut each quarter into 3 or 4 strips.

3. Heat half the oil in wok or skillet. Add abalone, stir-fry 1 minute, remove; keep warm.

4. Heat remaining oil in wok, add mushrooms, onions, pepper, cucumber and gingerroot, stir-fry 1 minute. Add combined sauces, vinegar, sugar, crumbled bouillon cube, water, sesame oil and blended cornstarch and sherry. Stir until sauce boils and thickens. Add abalone, stir until heated through.
Serves 4.

Squid with Broccoli

YOU WILL NEED

2lb squid
1/2 cup vegetable oil
2 onions, quartered
2 stalks celery
2lb broccoli
2 teaspoons grated fresh gingerroot
1/2 cup water
2 chicken bouillon cubes
1/4 cup oyster-flavored sauce
4 teaspoons light soy sauce
1/2 teaspoon Oriental sesame oil
1/2 teaspoon sugar
4 teaspoons cornstarch
3 tablespoons dry sherry
4 green onions

Note: Recipe can be prepared several hours ahead. Stir-fry just before serving.

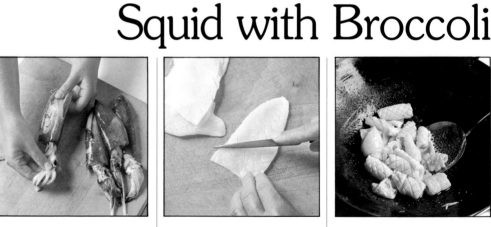

1. Hold squid firmly with one hand. With the other hand, hold head and pull gently. Head and inside of body of squid will come away in one compact piece. Remove bone which will be found at open end of squid; it looks like a piece of plastic. Clean squid under cold water, then rub off outer skin. (Some seafood stores have cleaned squid available.)

2. Cut squid lengthways down center. Spread squid out flat with the inside surface facing upwards. Using sharp knife score shallow diagonal slashes in diamond pattern on squid surface; this helps tenderize squid and makes it curl during cooking.

3. Heat oil in wok or skillet, add squid, stir-fry until it curls, remove from wok; drain on absorbent paper. Add onions, celery, broccoli and gingerroot to wok, stir-fry 3 minutes. Stir in combined water, crumbled bouillon cubes, sauces, sesame oil, sugar and blended cornstarch and sherry; stir until sauce boils. Return squid to wok, stir until heated through. Serve topped with green onions.
Serves 4.

Crab-Stuffed Shrimp

YOU WILL NEED
2lb uncooked jumbo shrimp
all-purpose flour
2 eggs
3 tablespoons milk
fresh white bread crumbs
oil for deep-frying

CRAB STUFFING
6oz can crab meat
¼ cup finely chopped mixed Chinese pickles ,
4 green onions, finely chopped
1 stalk celery, finely chopped
1 egg white
2 teaspoons cornstarch
1 teaspoon dry sherry
1 teaspoon light soy sauce

SPICY SAUCE
¼ cup vegetable oil
1 large onion, finely chopped
1 tablespoon curry powder
3 tablespoons sate sauce
2 teaspoons light soy sauce
4 teaspoons dry sherry
1 teaspoon sugar
½ cup heavy cream

1. Shell and devein shrimp, leaving tails intact. Using sharp knife cut along back of shrimp, but do not cut right through. Gently pound shrimp flat.

2. With small spatula press about 1 rounded tablespoon of crab stuffing onto shrimp. Gently coat shrimp with flour. Make sure to keep shrimp crab-side-up as stuffing could fall off shrimp. Using two forks, coat shrimp with combined beaten eggs and milk, then press bread crumbs firmly onto shrimp. Place shrimp in single layer on tray, refrigerate until ready to deep-fry. Deep-fry in batches in hot oil until golden brown and cooked through; drain on absorbent paper. Do not have oil too hot or crumbs will brown too quickly and shrimp will not cook through. Serve shrimp with spicy sauce.

Crab Stuffing: Drain crab, remove any fibrous tissue. Combine crab, pickles, onions, celery, egg white, cornstarch, sherry and sauce in bowl; mix well.

Spicy Sauce: Heat oil in pan, add onion, cook, stirring, until onion is soft. Add curry powder, cook 1 minute. Add sauces, sherry and sugar, cook, stirring, 2 minutes. Stir in cream, simmer, uncovered, about 2 minutes or until slightly thickened. Pour sauce into 4 individual serving bowls.
Serves 4 as an appetizer.

Note: Recipe can be prepared several hours ahead. Deep-fry just before serving.

Bamboo Shrimp

YOU WILL NEED
1lb uncooked jumbo shrimp
1 bamboo shoot
1 stalk celery
4 green onions
3 slices cooked ham
¼ cup vegetable oil
1 teaspoon grated fresh gingerroot
½ cup water
1 chicken bouillon cube
1 teaspoon cornstarch
2 teaspoons dry sherry

1. Shell and devein shrimp.

2. Cut bamboo shoot, celery, onions and ham evenly into ¼ inch strips.

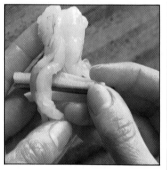

3. Cut a ½ inch slit right through shrimp, along the line of the vein. Push a strip of bamboo shoot, celery, onion and ham carefully through slit in each shrimp.

4. Heat oil in wok or skillet, add gingerroot, stir-fry until fragrant. Add shrimp, stir-fry until just cooked. Add combined water, crumbled bouillon cube and blended cornstarch and sherry, stir until sauce boils and thickens, simmer 1 minute.
Serves 4 as an appetizer.

Note: Recipe can be prepared several hours ahead. Stir-fry just before serving.

Rice with Crab

YOU WILL NEED
1½ cups long-grain rice
1 onion
6oz can crab meat
3 tablespoons vegetable oil
2 eggs
6 green onions, chopped
4 teaspoons light soy
sauce

1. Add rice to large pan of boiling water, boil, uncovered, 12 minutes; drain. Spread rice evenly over large shallow tray, refrigerate until cold.

Note: Rice best cooked a day ahead. Cook remaining recipe just before serving.

2. Grate onion. Drain crab meat, remove any fibrous tissue; flake crab.

3. Heat oil in wok or skillet, add onion, stir-fry until softened. Beat eggs, pour into wok over onion, stir lightly, cook until set. Remove from wok, cut omelet into large strips.

4. Add rice to wok, stir-fry until heated through. Add crab and green onions, stir-fry 1 minute. Add omelet strips and sauce, mix lightly; cook further minute.
Serves 4.

Chinese Fish

YOU WILL NEED
2 x 1lb whole fish
4 teaspoons grated fresh
gingerroot
2in piece fresh gingerroot,
extra
6 green onions
¼ cup light soy sauce
3 tablespoons vegetable oil

1. Clean and scale fish. Fill shallow pan two-thirds full of water. Add gingerroot, bring to boil, boil 5 minutes. Reduce heat, place fish in water, cover, simmer 10 minutes or until fish is cooked through.

2. Remove fish from pan; drain well. Place on heated serving plates. While fish is cooking, cut extra gingerroot into thin strips. Cut onions diagonally into thin slices.

3. Pour sauce over fish, sprinkle with gingerroot and onions. Heat oil in pan, pour over fish; serve immediately.
Serves 2.

Note: Recipe best made just before serving.

Shrimp Omelets

YOU WILL NEED
8 eggs
vegetable oil
2oz mushrooms,
  finely chopped
4 green onions,
  finely chopped
1 stalk celery,
  finely chopped
½lb cooked shrimp,
  shelled, chopped
8oz can bean sprouts,
  drained

SAUCE
4 teaspoons cornstarch
1 cup water
2 chicken bouillon cubes
1 teaspoon sugar
2 teaspoons light soy
  sauce

Note: Recipe can be prepared several hours ahead. Cook just before serving.

1. Beat eggs in small bowl until slightly frothy.

2. Heat small amount of oil in pan. Add mushrooms, cook,

stirring, 1 minute; drain. Add mushrooms to beaten eggs, stir in onions, celery, shrimp and bean sprouts; mix well.

3. Add enough oil to medium-sized skillet to just cover base. When oil is hot, pour omelet mixture into pan using cup to make 4 small omelets.

4. When mixture is firm on one side, separate omelets with spatula or egg slice. Turn, cook other side. Stack on warm plate while cooking remaining omelets; keep warm. To serve, stack omelets on plates, spoon over sauce.

Sauce: Blend cornstarch and water in pan, add crumbled bouillon cubes, sugar and sauce. Stir over heat until sauce boils and thickens.
Serves 4.

Butterfly Shrimp

YOU WILL NEED
1½lb uncooked jumbo
  shrimp
3 egg yolks
1½ teaspoons cornstarch
2 slices bacon
oil for deep-frying

Note: Recipe can be prepared several hours ahead. Deep-fry just before serving.

1. Shell and devein shrimp, leaving tails intact, rinse, pat dry. With sharp knife, cut deep slit along back of each shrimp, taking care not to cut right through.

2. Press cut-side gently with fingers to flatten.

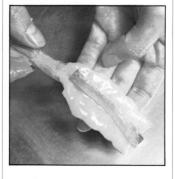

3. Beat egg yolks and cornstarch together in small

bowl. Cut bacon into 2 inch x ½ inch strips. Dip shrimp into egg yolk mixture. Place a strip of bacon on cut side of shrimp.

4. Deep-fry shrimp in batches in hot oil until golden brown; drain on absorbent paper. Serves 4 as an appetizer.

Crab in Gingerroot Sauce

YOU WILL NEED
2 cooked crabs
8 green onions
4in piece fresh gingerroot
¼ cup vegetable oil
½ teaspoon Oriental sesame oil
1 small red bell pepper, thinly sliced
½ cup water
3 tablespoons dry sherry
2 teaspoons light soy sauce
1 chicken bouillon cube
1 teaspoon sugar
2 teaspoons cornstarch
¼ cup water, extra

Note: Recipe can be prepared several hours ahead. Cook just before serving.

1. Wash crabs. Gently pull away round hard shell at top. With a small sharp knife gently cut away the grey fibrous tissue. Rinse again to clean crab.

2. Chop off claws and big nippers. Crack these lightly with back of cleaver to break through the hard shell. This makes it easier to eat the crab meat. Chop down center of crab to separate body into 2 halves. Cut each half evenly into 3 pieces.

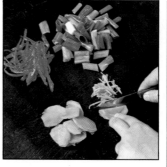

3. Cut onions into 1 inch lengths. Cut gingerroot into very thin strips.

4. Heat oil and sesame oil in wok or skillet, add gingerroot, stir-fry until fragrant. Add crab, stir-fry 1 minute. Stir in pepper, water, sherry, sauce, crumbled bouillon cube and sugar, simmer, covered, 4 minutes. Add blended cornstarch and extra water, stir until sauce boils and coats crab well. Add green onions, simmer, uncovered, 1 minute.
Serves 6.

Braised Shrimp with Vegetables

YOU WILL NEED
1lb uncooked jumbo shrimp
15oz can straw mushrooms
8oz can bamboo shoots
4 teaspoons vegetable oil
½lb broccoli, chopped
1 teaspoon oyster-flavored sauce
⅛ teaspoon sugar
½ teaspoon grated fresh gingerroot
1 teaspoon cornstarch
½ cup chicken broth

Note: If straw mushrooms are not available, substitute canned champignons (small whole mushrooms). Recipe best made just before serving.

1. Shell and devein shrimp.

2. Drain mushrooms. Drain bamboo shoots, cut evenly into thin slices.

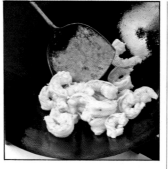

3. Heat oil in wok or skillet, add shrimp, stir-fry until just cooked; remove from wok.

4. Add bamboo shoots, mushrooms and broccoli to wok, stir-fry until broccoli is just tender. Stir in shrimp with combined sauce, sugar, gingerroot and blended cornstarch and broth, stir until mixture boils and thickens.
Serves 4.

Sweet and Sour Pork

YOU WILL NEED
2 teaspoons sugar
¼ cup light soy sauce
4 teaspoons dry sherry
1 egg yolk
2½lb lean pork chops
1 red bell pepper
cornstarch
oil for deep-frying
15¼oz can pineapple
chunks
¼ cup vegetable oil, extra
1 large onion, sliced
8 green onions, sliced
¼lb mushrooms, sliced
1 medium cucumber
2 stalks celery, sliced
1 cup water
3 tablespoons tomato
ketchup
1 chicken bouillon cube
2 tablespoons cornstarch,
extra
¼ cup white vinegar

Note: Pork can be marinated, and sauce made several hours ahead. Deep-fry pork and add to heated sauce just before serving.

1. Combine sugar, half the sauce, sherry and egg yolk in bowl, mix well. Trim pork, discard fat and bones. Cut pork into 1 inch cubes, add to sauce mixture; mix well. Cover, stand 1 hour, stirring occasionally. Cut pepper into thick slices.

2. Remove pork from marinade, reserve marinade. Toss pork lightly in cornstarch. Deep-fry pork in batches in hot oil until golden brown and cooked through; drain on absorbent paper.

3. Drain pineapple, reserve syrup. Heat extra oil in wok or skillet, add vegetables, stir-fry 3 minutes. Add reserved pineapple syrup, reserved marinade, remaining sauce, water, ketchup, crumbled bouillon cube and blended extra cornstarch and vinegar, stir until sauce boils and thickens. Add pineapple and pork, stir until combined.
Serves 4 to 6.

Spiced Pork

YOU WILL NEED
3lb lean pork chops
½ teaspoon five-spice
powder
2 tablespoons sweet sherry
2 tablespoons cornstarch
3 tablespoons light soy
sauce
1 teaspoon finely chopped
fresh gingerroot
oil for shallow-frying
¼ cup water
1 chicken bouillon cube
2 teaspoons light soy
sauce, extra
Chinese mixed pickles

1. Trim pork, discard fat and bones. Combine five-spice powder, sherry, cornstarch, sauce and gingerroot in large bowl, add pork; mix well. Refrigerate 2 hours, stirring occasionally. Shallow-fry pork in hot oil until golden brown and just cooked through; drain on absorbent paper.

3. Cut pork into serving-sized pieces; keep warm.

4. Combine water, crumbled bouillon cube and extra sauce in pan, bring to boil, pour over pork. Top with pickles. (If preferred, you can make your own pickles using our recipe on page 112.)
Serves 4.

Note: Pork can be marinated several hours ahead. Cook just before serving.

Barbequed Pork Ribs

YOU WILL NEED

**2lb country-style pork ribs
    or sliced pork belly**
⅓ cup barbeque sauce
**4 teaspoons Chinese chili
    sauce**
**3 tablespoons light soy
    sauce**
⅓ cup honey
⅓ cup brown vinegar
**¼ teaspoon five-spice
    powder**
⅓ cup dry sherry
1 clove garlic, minced
**1 tablespoon grated fresh
    gingerroot**

1. Add pork to large pan of water, bring to boil, cover, simmer 20 minutes; drain.

2. Place pork in roasting pan. Combine sauces, honey, vinegar, five-spice powder, sherry, garlic and gingerroot in jug; mix well. Pour over pork, stand 1 hour, turning pork occasionally.

3. Bake pork in 375°F oven about 1 hour or until tender, basting frequently.
Serves 4 to 6.

Note: *Recipe can be prepared a day ahead. Bake just before serving.*

Trotters with Gingerroot

YOU WILL NEED

4 pig's trotters
1½ cups brown vinegar
1½ cups sugar
**½lb fresh gingerroot,
    chopped**
**2 thin Chinese turnips,
    peeled, sliced**

1. Ask the butcher to cut the trotters into 2 inch pieces. Place trotters into large bowl, cover with cold water, stand 15 minutes; drain. Place trotters in large heavy-based pan, cover with with cold water. Bring to boil, cover, boil 1 minute; drain. Cover trotters again with cold water, bring to boil, cover, boil 1 minute; drain well.

2. Return trotters to pan, add vinegar, sugar and gingerroot, stir until combined. Bring to boil, cover, simmer 2 hours, stirring occasionally.

3. Add turnips to pan, cover, simmer further 1 hour. During last 15 minutes of cooking time, remove lid, increase heat slightly. Gingerroot sauce should be reduced enough to coat pig's trotters in thick glaze. Be careful as the reduced liquid could burn on base of pan. Stir occasionally during the last 15 minutes of cooking time.
Serves 4.

Note: *Recipe can be made several hours ahead.*

Steamed Pork Buns

YOU WILL NEED

3 cups all-purpose flour
1 tablespoon double-acting baking powder
2oz lard
¾ cup warm water
1 teaspoon white vinegar
vegetable oil

PORK FILLING

3 tablespoons vegetable oil
1 tablespoon grated fresh gingerroot
1 clove garlic, minced
4 teaspoons hoisin sauce
4 teaspoons oyster-flavored sauce
4 teaspoons light soy sauce
½ teaspoon Oriental sesame oil
1 tablespoon cornstarch
½ cup water
½lb Chinese barbequed pork, finely chopped
4 green onions, finely chopped

1. Sift flour and baking powder into bowl, rub in lard. Add combined warm water and vinegar, mix to a soft pliable dough. Turn dough onto lightly floured surface, knead lightly, cover; stand 20 minutes. Cut 12 x 5 inch squares of grease-proof paper, lightly brush one side of each square with oil. Knead dough lightly, shape evenly into 12 balls.

2. Roll balls of dough on floured surface to 4 inch rounds. Brush edges lightly with water. Place a round of dough in hand, top with 1 tablespoon of pork filling, press edges together to seal.

3. Pinch ends together firmly to form a ball. Repeat with remaining dough rounds and pork filling. Place buns, seam-side-down, on paper squares.

4. Choose a pan slightly smaller than the diameter of the steamer. Fill pan about one-third full of water, bring to boil. Arrange buns on paper in single layer in steamer. If using steamer with two or three racks, fill remaining racks. Place racks on top of first rack. Steam buns, covered, over gently boiling water 20 minutes. There is no need to change position of racks during cooking time. The steamer can also be placed in a wok partly filled with boiling water; make sure water is below base of steamer.

Pork Filling: Heat oil in skillet, add gingerroot and garlic, cook, stirring, until fragrant. Add sauces and sesame oil, simmer, stirring, 2 minutes. Stir in blended cornstarch and water, stir until sauce boils, simmer, uncovered, 2 minutes. Add pork and onions; cool to room temperature. Makes 12 buns.

Note: These buns are cooked in bamboo steamers, available at Asian stores. Chinese barbequed pork can bought at Asian food stores, or make your own using our recipe on page 50. Pork filling can be made 3 days ahead. Buns can be prepared several hours ahead. Steam buns just before serving.

Pork Ribs with Chili Plum Sauce

YOU WILL NEED
1½lb country-style pork
    ribs or sliced pork belly
1 tablespoon canned
    black beans
4 teaspoons oyster-
    flavored sauce
4 teaspoons dark
    soy sauce
3 tablespoons dry sherry
1½ teaspoons five-spice
    powder
½ teaspoon ground
    pepper
CHILI PLUM SAUCE
2 teaspoons vegetable oil
1 clove garlic, minced
½ teaspoon grated fresh
    gingerroot
2 green onions, chopped
⅔ cup bottled plum sauce
½ teaspoon chili sauce
2 teaspoons light soy
    sauce
1 chicken bouillon cube
2 teaspoons cornstarch
⅓ cup water

1. Using sharp knife, remove excess fat from ribs.

Note: Chili Plum Sauce can be made several hours ahead. Broil ribs just before serving.

2. Cover black beans with water in bowl, stand 15 minutes. Drain beans, mash with fork. Combine black beans, sauces, sherry, five-spice powder and pepper. Coat ribs with black bean mixture, place on rack over shallow roasting pan. Broil, turning occasionally, 10 minutes.

3. Brush ribs with chili plum sauce, broil further 5 minutes or until golden brown and cooked through. Serve with remaining sauce.

Chili Plum Sauce: Heat oil in pan, add garlic, gingerroot and onions, cook, stirring, 1 minute. Stir in combined sauces, crumbled bouillon cube and blended cornstarch and water, stir until sauce boils and thickens.

Serves 6.

Pork and Chicken with Black Beans

YOU WILL NEED
3 pork tenderloins
2 boneless, skinless
    chicken breast halves
3 egg whites
2 tablespoons cornstarch
oil for deep-frying
2 green onions, sliced
½ red bell pepper, sliced
BLACK BEAN SAUCE
3 tablespoons canned
    black beans
1 clove garlic, minced
2 tablespoons grated fresh
    gingerroot
1 teaspoon Chinese chili
    sauce
4 teaspoons oyster-
    flavored sauce
2 tablespoons light soy
    sauce
1 teaspoon Oriental
    sesame oil
4 teaspoons dry sherry
1 teaspoon sugar
2 teaspoons cornstarch,
    extra
⅔ cup water
1 chicken bouillon cube

1. Cut pork and chicken into ½ inch x 3 inch strips.

Note: Black Bean Sauce can be made several hours ahead. Deep-fry pork and chicken just before serving.

2. Combine egg whites and cornstarch in bowl; mix well. Add pork and chicken strips a few at a time; stir to coat. Deep-fry strips in batches in hot oil until golden brown and just cooked through; drain on absorbent paper.

3. Add pork and chicken to black bean sauce, stir until heated through. Serve topped with onions and pepper.

Black Bean Sauce: Soak black beans in water in bowl 30 minutes, rinse; drain well. Blend black beans, garlic, gingerroot, sauces, sesame oil, sherry and sugar until smooth. Stir black bean mixture in wok over low heat until mixture boils. Stir in blended cornstarch, water and crumbled bouillon cube, stir until sauce boils and thickens.

Serves 4 to 6.

Spiced Chicken

YOU WILL NEED
1 cup light soy sauce
2 tablespoons grated fresh
gingerroot
2 cloves garlic, minced
4 teaspoons five-spice
powder
2 x 3lb chickens
oil for deep-frying

SPICE MARINADE
3 tablespoons honey
3 tablespoons dry sherry
½ teaspoon five-spice
powder
½ teaspoon Oriental
sesame oil
4 teaspoons dark soy
sauce

FRIED SALT AND PEPPER
¼ cup salt
½ teaspoon ground white
pepper
1 teaspoon five-spice
powder

1. Fill a very large boiler three-quarters full with water, add sauce, gingerroot, garlic and five-spice powder. Place lid on boiler, bring water to boil, boil 2 minutes. Add whole chickens, bring to boil, boil 1 minute, remove from heat. Stand chickens in liquid, covered, until liquid is just warm. Remove chickens from liquid; drain well.

2. Using cleaver or very sharp, large knife, cut chicken in half through center of breast bone and back bone; drain any excess liquid from chickens.

3. Place chickens, cut-side-down, on 2 baking sheets. Rub marinade into skin of chickens (use all marinade); stand 2 hours. Rub marinade occasionally into chicken skin.

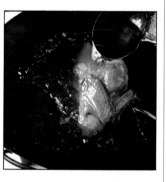

4. Deep-fry one chicken half in hot oil until golden brown and cooked through, spooning oil over chicken constantly; drain on absorbent paper, keep warm. Repeat with remaining chicken. Cut chicken into serving-sized pieces with cleaver or knife. Serve with fried salt and pepper for dipping.

Spice Marinade: Combine all ingredients in bowl; mix well.

Fried Salt and Pepper: Place salt and pepper in skillet, cook, stirring, 2 minutes. Add five-spice powder, cook, stirring, 1 minute. Spoon into small flat bowls.
Serves 8.

Note: *Recipe best prepared on day of serving. Deep-fry just before serving.*

Chicken with Mangoes

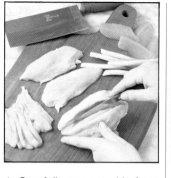

YOU WILL NEED
- 3 whole chicken breasts
- 8 green onions
- 15oz can sliced mangoes, drained
- oil for deep-frying
- 3 tablespoons vegetable oil, extra
- 2in piece fresh gingerroot, thinly sliced
- ¾ cup water
- 4 teaspoons light soy sauce
- 1 teaspoon Oriental sesame oil
- 3 tablespoons white vinegar
- 2 teaspoons sugar
- 2 chicken bouillon cubes
- 2 teaspoons cornstarch
- 3 tablespoons dry sherry

BATTER
- ¾ cup all-purpose flour
- ¼ cup self-rising flour
- 1 cup cold water

1. Carefully remove skin from chicken. Using sharp knife, cut chicken from breasts to make 6 fillets. Cut chicken into ½ inch thick slices. Cut onions into ½ inch diagonal slices. Cut drained mangoes into ½ inch slices.

2. Place chicken in batter; mix well. Deep-fry chicken in batches in hot oil until golden brown; drain on absorbent paper. Heat extra oil in wok or skillet, add gingerroot, stir-fry until fragrant. Add combined water, sauce, sesame oil, vinegar, sugar, crumbled bouillon cubes and blended cornstarch and sherry, stir until sauce boils, simmer 3 minutes. At the last minute, add chicken, mangoes and onions, simmer 3 minutes; serve immediately.

Batter: Sift dry ingredients into bowl, gradually add water; mix to a smooth batter, whisk 3 minutes. Cover, stand 30 minutes, whisk again just before using.
Serves 4 to 6.

Note: Recipe can be prepared several hours ahead. Cook just before serving.

Chicken and Almonds

YOU WILL NEED
- 8 boneless, skinless chicken breast halves
- 1 teaspoon cornstarch
- 1 egg white, lightly beaten
- 2 tablespoons dry sherry
- oil for deep-frying
- 3 tablespoons vegetable oil, extra
- 2oz blanched almonds
- 1 teaspoon grated fresh gingerroot
- 1 large carrot, chopped
- ¼lb mushrooms, sliced
- ½ x 8oz can bamboo shoots, sliced
- 3 stalks celery, sliced
- 6 green onions, chopped

SAUCE
- 1½ cups water
- 4 teaspoons light soy sauce
- 1 chicken bouillon cube
- 4 teaspoons cornstarch
- 4 teaspoons dry sherry

1. Cut chicken into 1 inch pieces, combine with cornstarch, egg white and sherry in bowl; mix well.

2. Deep-fry chicken pieces in batches in hot oil until just cooked through; drain on absorbent paper. Heat extra oil in wok or skillet, add almonds, stir-fry until golden brown; drain on absorbent paper.

3. Add gingerroot and carrot to wok, stir-fry 1 minute. Add remaining vegetables, stir-fry until just tender. Add chicken and sauce, stir until mixture boils, stir in almonds.

Sauce: Combine water, sauce, crumbled bouillon cube and blended cornstarch and sherry in pan, stir over heat until mixture boils.
Serves 4 to 6.

Note: Recipe can be prepared several hours ahead. Cook just before serving.

Gingerroot and Onion Chicken

YOU WILL NEED
3lb chicken
2in piece fresh gingerroot, sliced
⅓ cup vegetable oil
3 tablespoons grated fresh gingerroot, extra
8 green onions

1. Wash chicken, place in large pan, cover with cold water, add gingerroot. Cover, bring to boil, simmer about 40 minutes or until tender. Cool chicken in liquid.

2. Drain chicken, refrigerate until firm. Cut chicken into small serving-sized pieces.

3. Combine oil, extra gingerroot and finely chopped onions in screw-top jar, shake well; refrigerate several hours. Shake again before using. To serve, spoon gingerroot mixture over chicken, top with extra green onions, if desired. Serves 4 to 6.

Note: Recipe can be prepared a day ahead.

Gingerroot Garlic Chicken

YOU WILL NEED
6oz Chinese egg noodles
3lb chicken
cornstarch
oil for shallow-frying
⅓ cup vegetable oil, extra
1 tablespoon light soy sauce
2 cloves garlic, minced
2 teaspoons grated fresh gingerroot
1 large onion, chopped
1 chicken bouillon cube
1 tablespoon light soy sauce, extra
1 teaspoon white vinegar
¼ cup tomato ketchup
¼ teaspoon sugar
1 teaspoon cornstarch, extra
½ cup water
3 green onions, finely shredded

1. Add noodles to pan of boiling water, boil, uncovered, until noodles are tender; drain. Rinse under cold water; drain noodles well.

2. Cut chicken into small serving-sized pieces. Toss chicken in cornstarch; shake away excess cornstarch. Shallow-fry chicken in batches in hot oil until golden brown and cooked through; drain on absorbent paper.

3. Heat half the extra oil in wok or skillet, add noodles and soy sauce, stir-fry until heated through. Spread noodles on serving plate; keep warm.

4. Heat remaining extra oil in wok, add garlic, gingerroot and onion, stir-fry until onion is transparent. Add chicken and combined crumbled bouillon cube, extra sauce, vinegar, ketchup, sugar and blended extra cornstarch and water. Stir until sauce boils and thickens and chicken is heated through; spoon over noodles. Top with green onions. Serves 4.

Note: Recipe can be prepared several hours ahead. Cook just before serving.

Hoisin Chicken

YOU WILL NEED
3lb chicken
cornstarch
oil for deep-frying
¼ cup vegetable oil, extra
1 tablespoon grated fresh
gingerroot
2 onions, chopped
½lb broccoli, chopped
1 red bell pepper, chopped
15oz can straw mush-
rooms, drained
3 tablespoons hoisin sauce
4 teaspoons light soy
sauce
3 tablespoons brown
vinegar
1 cup water
2 chicken bouillon cubes
½ teaspoon Oriental
sesame oil
1 tablespoon cornstarch,
extra
3 tablespoons dry sherry

Note: Recipe can be prepared several hours ahead. Cook just before serving.

1. Chop chicken into serving-sized pieces, toss chicken in cornstarch, shake away excess cornstarch. Deep-fry chicken in batches in hot oil until golden brown and cooked through; drain on absorbent paper. Heat extra oil in wok or skillet, add gingerroot, stir-fry until fragrant. Add onions, stir-fry 1 minute. Add broccoli, pepper and mushrooms, stir-fry 2 minutes.

2. Add combined sauces, vinegar, water, crumbled bouillon cubes, sesame oil and blended extra cornstarch and sherry, stir until boiling.

3. Add chicken, simmer further 2 minutes or until chicken is heated through.
Serves 4 to 6.

Chicken Chow Mein

YOU WILL NEED
½lb egg noodles
oil for deep-frying
4 boneless, skinless
chicken breast halves
1lb large uncooked shrimp
¼ cabbage
½lb lean pork, chopped
2 teaspoons light soy
sauce
2 teaspoons sherry
1 teaspoon cornstarch
⅓ cup vegetable oil, extra
1 tablespoon chopped
fresh gingerroot
1 clove garlic, minced
2 medium onions
1 red bell pepper
2 stalks celery
8 green onions, chopped
SAUCE
½ cup water
4 teaspoons light soy
sauce
2 chicken bouillon cubes
2 teaspoons cornstarch
4 teaspoons dry sherry

1. Add noodles to large pan of boiling water, boil, uncovered, until tender; drain. Rinse noodles under cold water; drain well. Spread noodles out on clean kitchen towel on wire rack. Stand at room temperature about 3 hours or until noodles are almost dry.

2. Deep-fry noodles in batches in hot oil until golden; drain on absorbent paper.

3. Chop chicken into cubes. Shell and devein shrimp, leaving tails intact. Shred cabbage. Combine chicken, pork, sauce, sherry and cornstarch in bowl; mix well. Cover, stand 1 hour.

4. Heat extra oil in wok or skillet, add gingerroot and garlic, stir-fry until fragrant. Add chicken and pork mixture, stir-fry until meat is almost cooked. Add shrimp, stir-fry 3 minutes. Add vegetables, stir-fry 2 minutes. Add sauce, stir until sauce boils and thickens. Serve chicken mixture with noodles.

Sauce: Combine water, sauce, crumbled bouillon cubes, cornstarch and sherry in jug.
Serves 6.

Note: Recipe can be prepared several hours ahead.

Beef with Cashews

YOU WILL NEED

1 lb boneless beef top
  sirloin steak
¼ cup vegetable oil
2 cloves garlic, minced
8 green onions, chopped
1 tablespoon chopped
  fresh gingerroot
3 oz unsalted roasted
  cashews
4 teaspoons cornstarch
½ cup water
2 teaspoons sate sauce
4 teaspoons light soy
  sauce
1 teaspoon Oriental
  sesame oil

1. Trim excess fat from beef, cut beef into ½ inch x 2 inch slices. Heat half the oil in wok or skillet, stir-fry beef in batches until well browned; remove beef from wok.

2. Heat remaining oil in wok, add garlic, onions, gingerroot and cashews, stir-fry about 1 minute or until onions are soft.

3. Add beef and blended cornstarch, water, sauces and sesame oil; stir until mixture boils and thickens.
Serves 4.

Note: *Recipe best made just before serving.*

Sherried Beef

YOU WILL NEED

1 lb piece beef tenderloin
3 tablespoons light soy
  sauce
3 tablespoons dry sherry
1 teaspoon sugar
½ teaspoon Oriental
  sesame oil
2 in piece fresh gingerroot
1 bunch (12 leaves) Swiss
  chard
3 tablespoons vegetable oil
3 tablespoons vegetable
  oil, extra
½ teaspoon cornstarch
¼ cup water
1 chicken bouillon cube

1. Remove all fat and sinew from beef. Cut beef into ¼ inch thick slices. Cut each slice in half, then pound out gently with a mallet. Place beef in bowl with sauce, sherry, sugar and sesame oil, cover, refrigerate 2 hours.

2. Cut gingerroot into wafer-thin slices. Wash Swiss chard, shake away excess water. Cut the thick white stalks into 1 inch slices. Cut leaves into large pieces.

3. Heat oil in wok or skillet, add stalks and gingerroot, stir-fry 3 minutes, remove from wok. Heat extra oil in wok, stir-fry beef in batches until browned. Return all beef to wok with blended cornstarch, water and crumbled bouillon cube, stir until mixture boils. Add Swiss chard leaves, stalks and gingerroot, simmer until Swiss chard leaves are wilted.
Serves 4 to 6.

Note: *Recipe can be prepared 6 hours ahead. Stir-fry just before serving.*

Gingerroot Beef

YOU WILL NEED

1lb piece beef tenderloin
2 teaspoons cornstarch
2 teaspoons vegetable oil
1 teaspoon dark soy sauce
¼lb fresh gingerroot,
**   thinly sliced**
3 tablespoons white
**   vinegar**
2 teaspoons sugar
3 tablespoons vegetable
**   oil, extra**
1 green bell pepper
6 green onions, sliced
1 fresh red chili pepper,
**   thinly sliced**

Note: *Recipe can be prepared several hours ahead. Stir-fry just before serving.*

1. Trim all fat and sinew from beef, cut beef into ¼ inch thick slices. Place beef in bowl, add blended cornstarch, oil and sauce; mix well. Stand 20 minutes. Combine gingerroot, vinegar and sugar in separate bowl, stand at least 20 minutes.

2. Heat extra oil in wok or skillet, add beef mixture in batches, spreading out beef slices in single layer. Brown on one side, turn to brown other side. Cook quickly and only until beef is just cooked, remove from wok.

3. Cut bell pepper in half, chop into 1 inch cubes.

4. Add gingerroot with liquid to wok with bell pepper and onions, stir-fry 3 minutes. Return beef to wok, stir-fry further minute. Serve topped with chili pepper.
Serves 4.

Beef Tenderloin Chinese-Style

YOU WILL NEED

1lb piece beef tenderloin
½ teaspoon baking soda
1 teaspoon sugar
1 teaspoon cornstarch
2 teaspoons dark soy
**   sauce**
1 teaspoon oyster-flavored
**   sauce**
2 teaspoons dry sherry
4 teaspoons vegetable oil
2 medium onions, sliced
4 teaspoons dry sherry,
**   extra**

Note: *Recipe can be prepared several hours ahead. Stir-fry just before serving.*

1. Trim fat and sinew from beef.

2. Cut beef into ¼ inch thick slices. Gently flatten with meat mallet or rolling pin. Place beef in bowl, add combined soda, sugar, cornstarch, sauces and sherry; mix well, cover, refrigerate 3 hours.

3. Heat oil in wok or skillet. Add onions, stir-fry until just golden brown. Transfer to heated serving plate.

4. Add beef mixture in batches to wok, spreading slices out in single layer. Brown on one side, turn to brown other side. Cook quickly and only until beef is just cooked. Add extra sherry; mix well. Serve beef over onions.
Serves 4.

VEGETABLES

Vegetables cooked in the Chinese style are crisp and colorful. Because cooking time is so short, they are full of flavor.

Chinese Vegetables

YOU WILL NEED

2 onions, quartered
1lb broccoli
¼ cup vegetable oil
4 teaspoons finely chopped fresh gingerroot
4 stalks celery, sliced
1 small bunch of Chinese cabbage or spinach, shredded
½lb snow peas
¾ cup water
2 chicken bouillon cubes
8 green onions, sliced

2. Heat oil in wok or large skillet, add onions, broccoli stalks and gingerroot; stir-fry 1 minute.

1. Separate onions into layers. Cut broccoli stalks into sticks, cut broccoli into flowerets.

3. Add broccoli flowerets, celery, cabbage and snow peas, stir-fry 1 minute.

4. Stir in water and crumbled bouillon cubes, cover, simmer about 3 minutes or until vegetables are just tender, stirring occasionally. Serve topped with green onions. Serves 4.

Note: Other vegetables, such as carrots, cauliflower, green beans, red or green bell peppers or zucchini, can be used in addition to, or in place of, those listed. Add these vegetables in Step 2. Recipe best made just before serving.

RICE AND NOODLES

Steamed rice is an essential accompaniment to any Chinese meal, or you may prefer Fried Rice. We tell you how to cook both perfectly and give you cooking methods for popular noodle dishes.

Fried Rice

YOU WILL NEED
3/4lb long-grain rice
3 slices bacon, finely
    chopped
vegetable oil
3 eggs, lightly beaten
3 tablespoons vegetable
    oil, extra
2 teaspoons grated fresh
    gingerroot
1/2lb cooked pork,
    thinly sliced
8 green onions,
    finely chopped
1lb cooked shrimp,
    shelled, deveined
2 teaspoons light soy
    sauce

1. Add rice gradually to large pan of boiling water; stir well. Boil, uncovered, about 12 minutes or until just tender; drain immediately in strainer, rinse well under cold running water; drain well.

2. Spread rice evenly over 2 baking sheets, refrigerate overnight, stirring occasionally. If serving the same day, spread on baking sheets, bake in 350°F oven about 20 minutes, stir every 5 minutes.

3. Fry bacon in wok until crisp, remove from wok. Heat a small quantity of oil in wok, pour in enough beaten eggs to make a thin omelet; turn, cook other side. Remove from wok, repeat with remaining eggs. Roll up omelets, cut into thin strips. Heat extra oil in wok, add gingerroot, stir-fry until fragrant. Add rice, stir-fry 5 minutes. Add omelet strips, bacon, pork, onions and shrimp, stir-fry until heated through; stir in sauce.

Note: *A cooked pork chop or Chinese barbequed pork can be used. Rice is best cooked a day ahead. Stir-fry just before serving.*

Vermicelli

YOU WILL NEED
**1 package rice vermicelli
oil for deep-frying**

1. Cut vermicelli bundle in half with scissors or sharp knife. Separate halves into bunches.

2. Using tongs, carefully lower a bunch at a time into very hot, deep oil.

3. When vermicelli rise to the surface, remove immediately with tongs or slotted spoon; drain on absorbent paper, crush vermicelli lightly. (The cooking time should be about 4 or 5 seconds.)

Note: *Vermicelli, also known as transparent noodles, are used as a garnish, or decorative surround to many Chinese dishes. Recipe best made just before serving.*

Noodle Baskets

YOU WILL NEED
**2 packages fine egg
        noodles
oil for deep-frying**

1. Add noodles to large pan boiling water, boil, uncovered, until tender. Drain, rinse under cold running water; drain well.

3. Oil inside of medium size strainer (5 inch diameter). Line with a layer of noodles, approximately ½ inch thick. Press down well but not too firmly. Oil base of another strainer (4 inch or 5 inch diameter), press down lightly onto noodles in first strainer.

4. Holding handles of both strainers together firmly, carefully lower into very hot oil. Deep-fry until noodles are crisp and golden. (Cooking time depends on thickness of noodles and heat of oil.) Remove from oil, carefully separate strainers, being careful not to break noodles. If necessary, run top of round-bladed knife round edge of noodles to loosen. Turn remaining strainer up-side-down. Carefully knock out noodle basket. Repeat with remaining noodles.

Note: *Noodle baskets are an unusual and attractive way in which to serve Chinese food . Baskets can be made several days ahead, store, wrapped in plastic wrap, in refrigerator. Or they can be wrapped and frozen; they will keep in good condition for several weeks. To reheat, place in 325°F oven about 10 minutes or until heated through. Allow longer heating time if baskets have been frozen.*

Fried Noodles

YOU WILL NEED
½lb egg noodles
oil for deep-frying

1. Add noodles to large pan of boiling water, boil, uncovered, about 5 minutes or until tender. Separate with fork during cooking.

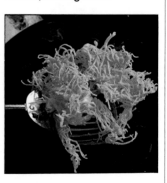

3. Using tongs, drop small amounts of noodles into hot oil, deep-fry until golden brown, turning once.

2. Drain noodles well; spread on tray lined with absorbent paper; allow to dry.

4. Remove noodles from oil; drain on absorbent paper. Repeat with remaining noodles. Serves 4 to 6.

Note: Noodles can be cooked several hours ahead. Deep-fry just before serving.

Steamed Rice

YOU WILL NEED
2 cups long-grain rice
water
¼ teaspoon salt

1. Wash rice well under cold running water. Place rice in pan, add sufficient cold water to come 1 inch above surface of rice (this applies to any quantity of rice). Stir in salt.

2. Bring to boil, boil, uncovered, until water begins to evaporate and steam holes appear in the rice.

3. Turn heat as low as possible, cover pan tightly, cook gently about 15 minutes or until tender. Remove from heat, stand 5 minutes, uncover; serve. Serves 6.

Note: Recipe best made just before serving.

DESSERTS

Chinese cuisine does not offer a wide range of desserts. We have included a few traditional recipes in this section and added some light and lovely desserts which make a superb ending to a Chinese meal.

Watermelon in Ginger Wine

YOU WILL NEED
½ watermelon
3 tablespoons superfine
    sugar
1 cup water
½ cup green ginger wine
2 pieces preserved
    gingerroot

3. Slice melon straight across, removing only the scooped-out portion of melon. Scoop out remaining melon.

1. With rounded side of melon baller facing up, press down firmly into melon.

4. Combine sugar, water and wine in pan, stir over heat until sugar is dissolved. Remove from heat, add gingerroot; cool. Pour syrup over watermelon, refrigerate several hours or overnight.
Serves 4.

2. Twist melon baller around, lift out melon ball; remove seeds if necessary. Continue until all the top of the melon has been scooped out.

Note: Any melon can be used in this recipe. Recipe can be made a day ahead.

Almond Jelly

YOU WILL NEED
**1 tablespoon unflavored
gelatin
¾ cup cold water
½ cup superfine sugar
¾ cup boiling water
1¼ cups evaporated milk
2 drops almond extract
2 kiwifruit, thinly sliced
4 strawberries**

3. Pour mixture into 4 dishes; cool. Cover, refrigerate until firm. Serve with kiwifruit and strawberries.
Serves 4.

1. Sprinkle gelatin over cold water in heatproof bowl, add sugar. Pour over boiling water, stir until sugar and gelatin are completely dissolved.

2. Add evaporated milk and extract; mix well.

Note: Recipe can be made a day ahead.

Banana Fritters

YOU WILL NEED
**2 cups self-rising flour
½ teaspoon baking soda
1½ cups water
4 bananas
all-purpose flour
oil for deep-frying**

1. Sift self-rising flour and soda into bowl, add water, mix to a smooth batter.

2. Peel bananas, cut into thirds. Roll banana pieces lightly in all-purpose flour.

3. Drop banana pieces into batter, drain away excess batter. Deep-fry in batches in hot oil until golden brown; drain on absorbent paper. Serve hot with ice cream.
Serves 4.

Note: Recipe best made just before serving.

Lychees and Mandarin Ice

YOU WILL NEED
1 cup superfine sugar
2 cups water
11oz can mandarin orange
segments
¼ cup fresh lemon juice
4 teaspoons Grand Marnier
20oz can lychees
11oz can mandarin orange
segments, extra

1. Combine sugar and water in pan, stir over low heat until sugar is dissolved. Bring to boil, boil, uncovered, 3 minutes; cool.

2. Blend or process 1 undrained can mandarins for 1 minute, push through sieve.

3. Add mandarin puree, juice and liqueur to sugar syrup, stir until combined. Pour into loaf pan, freeze until firm, stirring occasionally. Drain lychees and extra mandarin segments, reserve lychee syrup. Refrigerate lychees and mandarins until well chilled. Serve lychees and mandarins drizzled with some of the reserved lychee syrup, top with flaked mandarin ice.
Serves 4.

Note: Mandarin ice can be made 4 days ahead.

Melon with Champagne

YOU WILL NEED
1 large honeydew melon
½ cup superfine sugar
½ cup water
¼ cup green ginger wine
1lb green grapes
1 egg white, lightly beaten
superfine sugar, extra
1½ cups dry champagne,
chilled

1. Cut melon in half; remove seeds from each half. With melon baller, scoop out balls of melon, place into bowl. Cut remaining melon into pieces, reserve for another meal.

2. Combine sugar, water and wine in small pan, stir over low heat until sugar is dissolved. Bring to boil, boil, uncovered, 3 minutes; cool. Place syrup in bowl, cover, refrigerate until well chilled.

3. Cut bunches of grapes with stems large enough to hook over glasses. Brush grapes lightly with egg white to coat completely.

4. Place grapes immediately into bowl of sugar, sprinkle sugar over, coating all grapes evenly. Place grapes on tray, stand 2 hours. Place melon balls into 6 individual tall glasses, place grapes at side of glasses. Top with 1½ tablespoons of ginger syrup, pour over champagne.
Serves 4 to 6.

Note: When buying the grapes, choose small neat bunches. Recipe can be prepared several hours ahead. Assemble just before serving.

Hot Ice Cream Balls

YOU WILL NEED
4 pint carton vanilla ice cream
all-purpose flour
2 eggs
¼ cup milk
packaged unseasoned bread crumbs
oil for deep-frying
CARAMEL SAUCE
¼ cup (½ stick) butter
1 cup dark brown sugar, firmly packed
½ cup water
¼ cup Grand Marnier or Cointreau
4 teaspoons cornstarch
½ cup cream

3. Deep-fry ice cream balls in batches of 2 in hot oil about 30 seconds or until golden brown; drain on absorbent paper. Serve immediately with hot caramel sauce.

1. Put a metal tray into freezer 1 hour before starting. Scoop ice cream into balls with ice cream scoop, place on chilled tray, freeze until hard.

Caramel Sauce: Combine butter and sugar in pan, stir over heat until butter is melted. Add combined remaining ingredients, stir over low heat until sugar is dissolved, bring to boil, simmer, stirring, 3 minutes. Makes about 10.

2. Working very quickly, coat 1 or 2 ice cream balls lightly in flour, dip in combined beaten eggs and milk, then coat firmly with bread crumbs. Place immediately on tray in freezer; repeat with remaining ice cream balls working as above. Freeze balls until very hard.

Note: *It is important when making these ice cream balls to have everything as cold as possible. Ice cream must be very hard and should be a good quality full cream ice cream. The crumbed ice cream balls can be prepared several days ahead. Deep-fry just before serving.*

Gingered Junket

YOU WILL NEED
2 vanilla junket tablets
4 teaspoons cold water
3 tablespoons sugar
¼ cup dry whole milk
2 cups milk
1 teaspoon vanilla extract
ground nutmeg
preserved gingerroot with
**   syrup, sliced**

1. Crush junket tablets, dissolve in cold water in bowl.

2. Combine sugar and dry milk in bowl. Heat milk in pan until lukewarm (do not overheat), stir into dry milk mixture, stir in extract; mix well.

3. Add dissolved junket tablets, stir in quickly. Pour into 4 serving dishes, stand in warm place about 15 minutes or until set, refrigerate until cold. Sprinkle with nutmeg, top with gingerroot and a little gingerroot syrup.
Serves 4.

Note: Recipe can be prepared a day ahead; decorate just before serving.

Strawberry Sorbet

YOU WILL NEED
1 cup water
½ cup superfine sugar
3 tablespoons fresh lemon
**   juice**
3 tablespoons Grand
**   Marnier or Cointreau**
½lb strawberries
2 egg whites
¼ cup superfine sugar,
**   extra**

1. Blend water, sugar, juice, liqueur and strawberries on medium speed for 2 minutes.

2. Push mixture through a fine sieve into 7 inch x 11 inch baking pan; freeze until firm.

3. Beat egg whites in small bowl until soft peaks form, add extra sugar, beat until sugar is dissolved.

4. Remove frozen strawberry ice from freezer, flake with a fork; fold in egg white mixture. Freeze until firm, stirring occasionally.
Serves 4 to 6.

Note: The sorbet can be served alone or used as a topping for fruit. We have served it over chunks of well-chilled watermelon. Recipe can be made 4 days ahead.

...AND ALL THE LOVELY EXTRAS

These pages you will find full of interest – they have all the delightful odds and ends that add a special touch to a Chinese meal.

Honey Walnuts

YOU WILL NEED
¾ cup honey
4 teaspoons fresh lemon juice
1 teaspoon light soy sauce
½lb walnut halves
superfine sugar
oil for shallow-frying

2. Drain walnuts, toss in sugar to coat.

1. Combine honey, juice and sauce in bowl, add walnuts; mix well. Stand 2 hours, stirring occasionally.

3. Shallow-fry walnuts in hot oil until just golden; drain well.

Note: *These are delicious to serve with drinks or after-dinner coffee. Recipe best made on day of serving.*

Chocolate Gingerroot Lychees

YOU WILL NEED
16oz can lychees
2oz preserved gingerroot
6oz semisweet chocolate, chopped
1 tablespoon butter

1. Drain lychees, stand 1 hour on absorbent paper or until dry on surface, patting occasionally with the paper to make sure they are quite dry.

2. Cut gingerroot evenly into thin slivers.

3. Carefully fill each lychee with gingerroot.

4. Place chocolate and butter in top half of double saucepan, stir over simmering water until melted; cool slightly. Dip lychees into chocolate; carefully lift out with a fork. Tap fork gently on side of pan to remove excess chocolate. Place on baking paper-covered baking sheet. Refrigerate until set. Drizzle any remaining chocolate decoratively over top of each lychee. Keep refrigerated. Makes about 20.

Note: Recipe can be made a day ahead.

Chinese Custard Tarts

YOU WILL NEED
3 cups all-purpose flour
6oz lard
5 tablespoons hot water
CUSTARD
3 eggs
1/3 cup superfine sugar
1 1/2 cups milk
yellow food coloring

1. Sift flour into bowl, rub in lard.

3. Roll dough to 1/8 inch thickness. Cut rounds from dough using a 3 inch fluted cutter. Place rounds in lightly greased 12-hole cup cake pans (3 tablespoon capacity).

4. Pour custard carefully into pastry cases. Bake in 400°F oven 10 minutes, reduce heat to 375°F, bake further 10 minutes or until set.
Custard: Beat eggs and sugar in bowl, gradually add milk; add coloring if desired. Makes about 30.

2. Add hot water, mix to a firm dough. Knead gently on lightly floured surface.

Note: The yellow food coloring is optional, it gives the color characeristic of these tarts. Recipe can be made a day ahead.

Green Onion Curls

YOU WILL NEED
**1 bunch green onions
iced water**

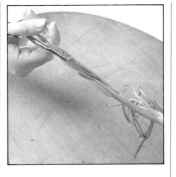

1. Choose young fresh green onions with fairly thick bulbs. Cut bulb from onion just where it starts to turn green, as shown in picture. (The bulbs can be used for cooking.) If onions are long, trim green tops, leaving about 4 inches.

2. With sharp scissors cut each green top down to where the hard stem starts. Make approximately 8 cuts in each.

3. Place onions in bowl of cold water with ice cubes. Refrigerate about 30 minutes or until onions curl. These make an attractive garnish for Chinese food.

Note: Onion curls can be made a day ahead, leave in iced water in refrigerator.

Gingered Cucumber

YOU WILL NEED
**2 cucumbers
½ teaspoon salt
¼ cup white vinegar
2 tablespoons sugar
1 teaspoon grated fresh
   gingerroot**

1. Using sharp knife, peel cucumbers, cutting as close to skin as possible. Run fork evenly down cucumbers.

2. Cut cucumbers into thin slices, place in bowl, sprinkle with salt; mix well. Stand cucumber 30 minutes; drain away excess liquid.

3. Combine remaining ingredients. Add to cucumber; mix well. Refrigerate several hours before serving.

Note: Recipe can be made a day ahead.

Sesame Peanut Candy

YOU WILL NEED
2 cups sugar
⅓ cup white vinegar
1 tablespoon water
**½ cup sesame seeds,
  toasted**
**1½ cups unsalted roasted
  peanuts**

3. Pour hot toffee evenly over seeds and nuts in pan.

1. Lightly oil 7 inch x 11 inch baking pan. Sprinkle half the seeds and all the nuts over base of prepared pan. Combine sugar, vinegar and water in small pan, stir over low heat until sugar is dissolved. Bring to boil; do not stir.

2. Boil 10 minutes or until golden brown. To test, add a little to cold water, it forms a hard ball when molded.

4. Smooth surface with the back of an oiled wooden spoon. Sprinkle remaining seeds over toffee; cool slightly. Cut candy into strips before it is completely cold.

Note: *To toast seeds, spread on baking sheet, bake in 350°F oven about 5 minutes or until golden. Recipe can be made 3 days ahead. Store in airtight container at room temperature.*

Chinese Mixed Pickles

YOU WILL NEED
1 large cucumber
1 red bell pepper
1 green bell pepper
4 stalks celery
4in piece fresh gingerroot
8 green onions
2 carrots
**1 large Chinese white
  radish or 2 turnips**
PICKLING LIQUID
2¼ cups sugar
2¼ cups white vinegar
1 teaspoon salt
1¼ cups water

1. Cut cucumber lengthways, remove seeds, cut into strips. Cut peppers into 1 inch squares. Slice celery diagonally. Slice gingerroot thinly. Slice green onions diagonally. Cut carrots and radish into thin strips.

2. Add vegetables to large pan of boiling water, remove from heat, stand vegetables in water 2 minutes.

3. Drain vegetables, pack firmly into hot sterilized jar or jars. Pour hot pickling liquid carefully into jar, making sure vegetables are completely covered, seal while hot; cool. Store in refrigerator 1 week before using.

Pickling Liquid: Combine all ingredients in pan, stir over low heat until sugar is dissolved, bring to boil; remove from heat.

Note: *Recipe can be made 2 months ahead. Store in refrigerator. To sterilize jar, wash jar in hot soapy water, rinse well. Stand jar right-way-up on baking sheet, place in 325°F oven 30 minutes.*

Fried Wontons

YOU WILL NEED
**1oz Chinese dried
mushrooms
1lb lean ground pork
1 cup finely chopped
uncooked spinach
4 teaspoons dry sherry
50 wonton skins
oil for deep-frying**
SWEET AND SOUR SAUCE
**½ cup white vinegar
1 cup canned pineapple
juice
2 teaspoons light soy
sauce
1 tablespoon tomato
ketchup
½ cup sugar
3 tablespoons cornstarch
¼ cup water
6½oz can or jar Chinese
mixed pickles, drained**

*Note: Wontons and sauce can be
prepared a day ahead; deep-fry
wontons and reheat sauce just
before serving.*

1. Place mushrooms in bowl,
pour over hot water, stand 30
minutes; drain. Remove
stems, chop mushrooms finely.
Combine mushrooms, pork,
spinach and sherry in bowl;
mix well. Place a teaspoon of
mixture in center of each skin,
brush edges of skins lightly
with water.

2. Gather edges of wonton
skins around filling, press
together firmly above filling to
form pouches.

3. Deep-fry wontons in
batches in hot oil until golden
brown; drain on absorbent
paper. Serve wontons with
sweet and sour sauce.

Sweet and Sour Sauce:
Combine vinegar, juice,
sauce, ketchup and sugar in
pan, bring to boil. Stir in
blended cornstarch and
water, stir until sauce boils and
thickens, simmer, uncovered,
3 minutes. Add sliced pickles,
simmer further 3 minutes.
Makes 50.

Bean Curd with Oyster Sauce

YOU WILL NEED
**½lb bean curd
3 tablespoons vegetable oil
3 stalks celery, sliced
6 green onions, chopped
1 red bell pepper, chopped
¼lb mushrooms, sliced
1 tablespoon cornstarch
½ cup water
3 tablespoons
oyster-flavored sauce
4 teaspoons light soy
sauce
4 teaspoons dry sherry**

*Note: Recipe can be prepared
several hours ahead. Stir-fry just
before serving.*

1. Cut bean curd into 1 inch
cubes.

2. Heat 1 tablespoon of oil in
wok or skillet, add bean curd,
stir-fry until lightly browned;
remove from wok.

3. Heat remaining oil in wok,
add vegetables, stir-fry 1
minute or until vegetables are
just tender.

4. Add bean curd to wok, stir-
fry lightly. Blend cornstarch
and water in jug, stir in sauces
and sherry. Add to wok, stir
until sauce boils and thickens.
Serves 4.

RESTAURANT SPECIALS

We asked some top restaurants to part with one of their favorite recipes.

Crab in Black Bean Sauce

YOU WILL NEED

2 medium cooked crabs
¼ cup black beans
1 tablespoon grated fresh gingerroot
2 cloves garlic, minced
¼ cup vegetable oil
3 tablespoons water
¼ cup vegetable oil, extra
¾ cup water, extra
1 chicken bouillon cube
2 teaspoons cornstarch
8 green onions, chopped

1. Wash crabs. Gently pull away round hard shell at top.

2. With small sharp knife gently cut away the grey fibrous tissue. Rinse with cold water to clean inside of crab.

3. Chop off claws and big nippers. Crack these lightly with back of cleaver to break through the hard shell. This makes it easier to eat the crab meat. Chop down center of crab to separate body into 2 halves, then chop across each half 3 times; this gives 6 body sections of crab.

4. Place beans into bowl of cold water; mix well. Stand 10 minutes. Drain, rinse beans well under cold running water. Place beans, gingerroot, garlic and oil into small bowl, mash well with fork until beans are finely crushed, add water; mix well. (Or blend or process the ingredients until lightly mashed.)

5. Heat extra oil in wok or skillet, add bean mixture, stir-fry 2 minutes. Add prepared crab, stir-fry 1 minute. Add ½ cup of extra water and crumbled bouillon cube, bring to boil, simmer, covered, 4 minutes. Add blended cornstarch and remaining water, stir until sauce boils and thickens and lightly coats the crab. Add onions just before serving. Serves 6.

Note: Recipe can be prepared several hours ahead. Stir-fry just before serving.

Billy Kee Chicken

YOU WILL NEED
3lb chicken
3 egg yolks, lightly beaten
oil for deep-frying
½ cup dry red wine
½ cup tomato ketchup
**1 teaspoon Worcestershire
    sauce**

Note: Recipe best made just before serving.

1. Cut chicken into serving-sized pieces; remove skin, cut chicken away from bones.

2. Chop chicken, combine with egg yolks; mix well.

3. Deep-fry chicken in batches in hot oil until lightly browned and just cooked through, remove from wok; drain on absorbent paper.

4. Drain oil from wok. Add combined wine, ketchup and sauce to wok, stir over heat until sauce boils. Stir in chicken pieces, simmer until heated through.
Serves 4 to 6.

Sizzling Steak

YOU WILL NEED
3 onions, quartered
1lb piece beef tenderloin
¼ cup water
¼ teaspoon baking soda
⅓ cup vegetable oil
**¼ cup Worcestershire
    sauce**
½ cup tomato ketchup
½ cup sugar
4 teaspoons dry white wine

Note: Recipe can be prepared 1 hour ahead. Stir-fry just before serving.

1. Separate layers of onion quarters. Slice beef thinly, flatten each piece with meat mallet. Combine beef with water and soda in bowl; mix well. Stand 1 hour; drain well. (This helps to tenderize the beef.)

2. Heat 4 teaspoons of the oil in wok or skillet, add beef, stir-fry 2 minutes to evaporate liquid; remove from wok. Pour oil from wok. Heat half the remaining oil in wok, return beef, stir-fry until well browned, remove from wok.

3. Heat cast iron steak plate in 450°F oven 10 minutes or until very hot. Heat remaining oil in wok, add onions, stir-fry quickly until golden brown and still crisp. Remove onions from wok, keep warm.

4. Return beef to wok, stir-fry 1 minute. Add combined sauce, ketchup and sugar, stir until sauce boils, simmer 2 minutes. Remove steak plate from oven, place on wooden base. Arrange onion on steak plate. Spoon beef mixture over onions. Pour wine over the steak plate immediately to give the characteristic sizzle.
Serves 4.

Flower Blossoms

YOU WILL NEED
2 cups all-purpose flour
1 egg, lightly beaten
¾ cup water,
   approximately
oil for deep-frying
FILLING
2oz Chinese dried
   mushrooms
½lb ground pork
1 small onion, finely
   chopped
3 green onions, chopped
½ x 8oz can water
   chestnuts, drained,
   finely chopped
4 teaspoons light soy
   sauce
4 teaspoons dry sherry
1 teaspoon grated fresh
   gingerroot

Note: Recipe can be prepared several hours ahead. Deep-fry just before serving.

1. Sift flour into bowl, add egg and enough water to mix to a stiff dough. Cut dough in half, roll out each half thinly on lightly floured surface to a 10 inch x 16 inch rectangle. Divide filling evenly into 2 portions, form each portion into a log down one side of dough rectangles.

2. Roll up from the longest edge to form neat rolls.

3. Cut each roll into 2 inch lengths, pinch edges together and roll into neat balls. Deep-fry balls in hot oil about 3 minutes or until golden brown and filling is cooked through; drain on absorbent paper.

Filling: Cover mushrooms with hot water in bowl, stand 30 minutes; drain. Remove stems, chop mushrooms finely. Combine mushrooms, pork, onion, green onions, water chestnuts, sauce, sherry and gingerroot in bowl; mix well.

Makes about 16.

Stuffed Chicken Wings

YOU WILL NEED
12 chicken wings
2 Chinese dried
   mushrooms
1 bamboo shoot
1 slice cooked ham
3 green onions
1 egg white, lightly beaten
oil for deep-frying
SAUCE
4 teaspoons tomato
   ketchup
2 teaspoons sugar
2 teaspoons light soy
   sauce
1 teaspoon Worcestershire
   sauce
¼ cup water

Note: Recipe can be prepared several hours ahead. Deep-fry just before serving.

1. Cut chicken tip and small drumstick off each chicken wing, leaving one thick piece from each wing. (These leftover chicken pieces can be used to make broth.)

2. Add wings to boiling water, boil 5 minutes, drain; cool. Make two light cuts on underside of each wing at both ends. Loosen meat from from bones with small sharp knife. With a twisting movement, remove bones.

3. Place mushrooms in bowl, cover with hot water, stand 30 minutes, drain; remove stems. Cut mushrooms, bamboo shoot, ham and onions into ¼ inch strips. Insert one strip of each ingredient into each chicken piece; trim ends neatly.

4. Dip chicken wings in egg white, deep-fry in hot oil until cooked through; drain on absorbent paper. Arrange on plate, pour over sauce.

Sauce: Combine all ingredients in pan, stir until mixture boils.

Honey Shrimp

YOU WILL NEED
1½lb uncooked jumbo shrimp
cornstarch
1 cup self-rising flour
1¼ cups water
1 egg, lightly beaten
oil for deep-frying
4 teaspoons vegetable oil, extra
3 tablespoons honey
sesame seeds

1. Shell and devein shrimp, toss in cornstarch, shake away excess cornstarch.

2. Sift flour into bowl, make well in center, gradually add combined water and egg; beat to a smooth batter. Add shrimp in batches to batter, mix well to coat shrimp.

3. Deep-fry shrimp in batches in hot oil until golden brown and cooked through; drain on absorbent paper.

4. Remove oil from wok, wipe wok clean. Heat extra oil in wok, add honey, stir over low heat until heated through. Add shrimp, toss to coat well. Serve sprinkled with seeds. Serves 4.

Note: Recipe best made just before serving.

Pork Chops with Plum Sauce

YOU WILL NEED
6 pork loin chops
1 tablespoon cornstarch
3 tablespoons dry sherry
4 teaspoons light soy sauce
4 teaspoons hoisin sauce
1 teaspoon Oriental sesame oil
1 teaspoon sugar
3 tablespoons vegetable oil
½ cup water
¾ cup bottled plum sauce
2 dried red chili peppers, finely chopped

1. Remove excess fat from chops, cut chops into large strips. Combine strips with blended cornstarch, sherry, sauces, sesame oil and sugar in bowl; mix well. Stand 1 hour.

2. Drain pork, reserve marinade. Heat oil in wok or skillet, add pork, stir-fry until golden brown; remove from heat.

3. Combine water, plum sauce, chili peppers and reserved marinade in pan, stir over high heat until boiling.

4. Add marinade mixture to pork in wok, stir until boiling, simmer, covered, 15 minutes. Serves 6.

Note: Recipe can be prepared several hours ahead. Cook just before serving.

Chicken Hot Pot

YOU WILL NEED
**1oz Chinese dried
  mushrooms**
4 green onions
3lb chicken
cornstarch
¼ cup vegetable oil
5 slices fresh gingerroot
1 clove garlic, minced
¼ cup chicken broth
½ cup dry white wine
**2 teaspoons cornstarch,
  extra**
**4 teaspoons light soy
  sauce**
½ cup chicken broth, extra

*Note: Recipe best made close
to serving.*

1. Place mushrooms in bowl,
cover with hot water, stand 30
minutes; drain. Trim mushroom stems. Cut onions into 2
inch lengths. Cut chicken into
small serving-size pieces,
coat well with cornstarch.

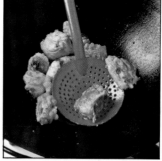

2. Heat oil in wok or skillet,
stir-fry chicken in batches until
golden brown. Return all
chicken to wok.

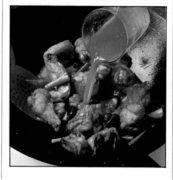

3. Add mushrooms, onions,
gingerroot and garlic to wok,
stir-fry 1 minute. Add combined broth, wine and blended
extra cornstarch and sauce.
Stir until mixture boils.

4. Place chicken mixture into
hot pot or ovenproof dish, add
extra broth. Bake, covered, in
350°F oven about 25 minutes
or until chicken is cooked.
Serves 6.

Toffee Apples

YOU WILL NEED
**2 medium size green
  apples**
oil for deep-frying
**2 teaspoons vegetable oil,
  extra**
1 cup water
2 cups sugar
**3 tablespoons sesame
  seeds**
Oriental sesame oil
BATTER
1 cup all-purpose flour
1 cup water
2 teaspoons vegetable oil

*Note: A wok is necessary when
making the toffee for this dessert.
Recipe best made just before
serving.*

1. Peel apples, cut into
quarters, remove cores. Cut
each quarter crossways in
half to make 16 pieces. Drop
apple into batter, drain away
excess batter. Deep-fry apple
in hot oil until lightly browned;
drain on absorbent paper.

2. Drain oil from wok. Heat
extra oil in wok, add water and
sugar, stir until boiling. Continue stirring rapidly over high
heat (a wide metal draining
spoon rather than a wooden
spoon is best for this). After
about 5 minutes stirring mixture will go white and foamy,
almost as if sugar has crys-
tallized. Continue stirring
rapidly another 5 minutes until
mixture becomes clear. Continue stirring further 3 minutes
or until toffee turns a light
golden color.

3. Remove from heat
immediately, add apples and
seeds, toss lightly to coat.
Turn immediately onto plate
which has been well greased
with sesame oil.

4. Using chopsticks. Pick up
toffee-coated apple, quickly
dip in bowl filled with iced
water and ice cubes. Serve
while hot.

Batter: Sift flour into bowl,
gradually add combined water
and oil, mix to a smooth batter.

Makes 16 pieces.

Wonton Skins

These paper-thin sheets of pastry can be used as skins for wontons, dumplings or egg rolls. For dumplings, cut pastry to same size as shown for wontons. For egg rolls, cut pastry into 8 inch squares.

YOU WILL NEED
2 cups all-purpose flour
¼ teaspoon salt
1 egg, lightly beaten
¾ cup water,
   approximately

Note: *Recipe can be made 2 days ahead; keep wrapped tightly in refrigerator. Suitable to freeze. If stacking wonton skins for later use, dust each skin lightly with flour before stacking.*

1. Sift flour and salt into bowl, add egg and enough water to mix to a stiff dough.

3. Roll dough on a well floured surface until paper thin.

2. If dough is too soft, add a little extra sifted flour for easier handling.

4. Using sharp knife, trim edges to form 15 inch x 15 inch square. Using a ruler, cut evenly into 3 inch squares. Place squares on baking sheet, cover with a damp cloth until ready to use.
Makes 25 wonton skins.

Chinese Tea

Chinese tea, one of the most thirst-quenching of all drinks, is available in many delicate and delightful flavors. Chilled, it makes a perfect iced tea, just gently crush a slice of orange or lemon over the glass of tea and add to tea.

Many people prefer to blend a little Chinese tea with a Ceylonese or Indian mixture. This gives a lightness and delicacy in flavor.

TO MAKE PERFECT CHINESE TEA

Chinese tea is taken weak, without milk or sugar. About one teaspoon of tea or less is used for ½ pint of boiling water.

Chinese tea can be made in a teapot or in a cup. When making it in a teapot, scald the pot first with boiling water, add the measured amount of tea and at once pour in the water, which should be at a full, rolling boil. As the boiling

water is added, the tea can be stirred. Cover, leave to steep for a few minutes. If you like your tea very weak, add extra boiling water to pot.

When making the tea directly in the cup, rinse cup with hot water, add the tea leaves and pour on the boiling water.

When the tea is drunk, more boiling water can be poured onto the same tea leaves in the cup. Many consider this second cup the better of the two – it is lighter and more delicate in flavor.

DIFFERENT TYPES

Chinese tea may be classified into the following: scented, black, green, white, Oolong. Each comprises many varieties, each with their own special characteristics which are further sorted and graded according to quality.

Scented tea: is manufactured from green tea which is fully dried then lightly scented with fragrant flowers. It possesses not only the characteristics of green tea but also the pleasant, light flower fragrance. Scented tea is named after the flower with which the tea is scented – jasmine, rosebud, orange bud or white chrysanthemum.

Black tea: is a fermented tea. During the manufacture it undergoes a chemical change whereby the green leaves are turned red, then black after being dried, thereby gaining its name.

Keemun black tea: is tightly and finely rolled and has won a wide reputation for a full, sweet flavor.

Yunnan black tea: is China's high-grown black tea. It contains a large proportion of pekoe with golden tips. Fresh and strong in taste it is fragrant

in aroma. (Pekoe is a grade of tea not a variety. Originally the pekoe quality was grown in Pekoe, in Southern China. Today most of it comes from Sri Lanka.)

Lapsang souchong: a special kind of black tea, is one of the most popular of all Chinese teas and well suited to Western tastes.

Green tea: is manufactured without going through the process of fermentation; the natural emerald green color of the fresh leaves is preserved.

White tea: a kind of unfermented tea, its manufacture is different from that of green tea. It is a special product of Shui Chi, Ching Wo and Sung Chi districts in Fukien province.

Oolong tea: is a semi-fermented tea, fragrant in aroma, with a delicious aftertaste.

GLOSSARY

Here are some names, terms and alternatives to help everyone use and understand our recipes.

ABALONE: is a frozen or canned mollusc, available from Asian food stores.

APPLES: we used Granny Smith apples.

ASPARAGUS TIPS: canned asparagus spears.

BAKING POWDER, DOUBLE-ACTING: is a rising agent consisting of an alkali and acid. It is mostly made from cream of tartar and baking soda in the proportion of 1 level teaspoon of cream of tartar to ½ level teaspoon of baking soda. This is equivalent to 2 level teaspoons double-acting baking powder.

BAMBOO SHOOTS: are available in cans.

BAMBOO STEAMERS: available in varying sizes. The base should be soaked in cold water for 10 minutes before using.

BEANS

Black Beans: are fermented, salted, soy beans. We used both canned and dried; one can be substituted for the other. Drain and rinse the canned variety. Leftover beans will keep for months in an airtight container in the refrigerator. Mash beans when cooking to release flavor.

Green Beans: should be topped and tailed before use.

Bean Curd: is also known as tofu. It is made from boiled, crushed soy beans to give a type of milk. A coagulant is added, much like the process of cheese making. We used firm tofu in this book. Buy it as fresh as possible; store any leftover tofu in refrigerator under water, which must be changed daily.

Bean Sprouts: we used mung bean sprouts in this book.

BEEF: we used several different cuts; usually the tender cuts such as tenderloin or top sirloin are ideal for quick cooking. If the recipe requires the beef to be sliced finely, freeze the piece at least 30 minutes before cutting. Cut across the grain of beef, for maximum flavor and moisture retention during cooking.

BREAD CRUMBS: can be unseasoned packaged or fresh bread crumbs. For fresh bread crumbs, use day-old bread made into crumbs by grating, blending or processing. One cannot be substituted for the other.

BUTTER: use salted or unsalted butter or substitute depending on your diet.

CHICKEN BROTH: homemade broth will give you the best flavor, but if you want to use bouillon cubes for convenience, use 1 crumbled bouillon cube to every 2 cups water.

CHILIES (fresh and dried): are available in many different types and sizes. The small ones (bird's eye or bird peppers) are the hottest. Use tight rubber gloves when chopping fresh chilies as they can burn your skin. The seeds are the hottest part so remove them if you want to reduce the heat content of recipes.

CHINESE MIXED PICKLES: a variety of fruit and vegetables preserved in vinegar, sugar and salt. The ingredients in the jar we used were gingerroot, green onions, papaya, cucumbers, carrots, chili and pears.

CHINESE TURNIP/CHINESE WHITE RADISH: also known as daikon. A basic food in some Asian countries.

CINNAMON: a fragrant bark used as a spice in ground form or sticks (quills).

CLEAVER: broad-bladed chopper available in many sizes and types. Cleavers are inexpensive and take only a little practice to use efficiently. Steel cleavers need to be wrapped in an oiled cloth to prevent them from rusting; keep them razor sharp by sharpening on an oilstone.

COINTREAU: an orange-flavored liqueur.

COLORINGS: we used concentrated liquid vegetable food colorings.

CORN: baby corn are small corn cobs canned in brine. Creamed corn is a type of puree in cans.

CORNSTARCH: is the main thickening ingredient used in Chinese cooking. It is always blended with a liquid before being added to other ingredients and boiled.

FIVE-SPICE POWDER: is a pungent mixture of ground spices which include cinnamon, cloves, fennel, star anise and Szechuan peppers.

FLOUR: we used several kinds of flour in this book. One cannot be substituted for another to give the same result.

Self-Rising Flour: substitute all-purpose flour and double-acting baking powder in the proportion of 1 cup all-purpose flour to 2 level teaspoons double-acting baking powder, sift together several times before using.

GINGERROOT

Fresh Gingerroot: scrape away skin and gingerroot is ready to grate, slice or chop. Keep peeled fresh gingerroot covered with sherry in a jar; store in refrigerator.

Ground Gingerroot: is also available but should not be substituted for fresh gingerroot in any recipe.

Preserved Gingerroot: is fresh gingerroot preserved in syrup.

GRAND MARNIER: orange-flavored liqueur.

GREEN GRAPES: we used seedless grapes.

HIBACHI: Japanese in origin; it is a deep container designed to hold burning coals; it is used for heating and cooking.

JUNKET TABLET: rennet tablet used for setting milk desserts.

LARD: is the fat obtained from melting down and clarifying pork fat.

LETTUCE: we used crisp iceberg lettuce.

LYCHEES: are small round fruit with a rough red skin, soft white flesh and a large brown seed. Peel rough skin, discard seed. Lychees are available canned.

MANDARIN ORANGE SEGMENTS: are canned in a light syrup.

MANGOES: we used cheeks of mangoes canned in a light syrup.

MILK: we used full cream homogenized milk, where specified. Evaporated milk is fresh cows' milk with 60% of the water removed by evaporation. Dry whole milk is made from cows' milk from which all the water is removed.

MUSHROOMS: we used both fresh and Chinese dried mushrooms. Chinese dried mushrooms have a unique flavor; soak them first in hot water, about 30 minutes, drain, discard stems, use caps as directed. Straw mushrooms are available in cans (champignons can be substituted).

NUTMEG: is the sweet smelling seed of the fruit of a South East Asian tree; it is available in ground form or you can grate your own with a fine grater.

OIL: vegetable oil or peanut oil can be used in Chinese cooking.

PEANUTS: unsalted roasted peanuts.

PORK: we used many cuts of pork; tender cuts such as pork tenderloins are ideal for quick cooking. Barbequed pork is roasted pork tenderloin available from Asian food stores.

PUFF PASTRY: is available frozen in blocks and ready rolled sheets.

RICE: we used long-grain white rice in this book.

SAUCE

Barbeque Sauce: is based on tomatoes, sugar and vinegar.

Chili Sauce: we used a hot Chinese variety consisting of chilies, salt and vinegar.

Hoisin Sauce: is a thick, sweet Chinese barbeque sauce made from salted black beans, onions and garlic.

Oyster-Flavored Sauce: is a rich brown sauce made from oysters cooked in salt and soy sauce, then thickened with different types of starches.

Plum Sauce: is a dipping sauce which consists of plums preserved in vinegar sweetened with sugar and flavored with chilies and spices.

Sate Sauce: also known as sata sauce; is a spicy sauce based on soy sauce, it contains sugar, oil, chili, onion, garlic and shrimp. Available from Chinese food stores.

Soy Sauce: is made from fermented soy beans.

Worcestershire Sauce: is a spicy sauce used mainly on red meat.

SEA SCALLOPS: we used sea scallops with coral attached.

SESAME OIL, ORIENTAL: made from roasted crushed white sesame seeds; is an aromatic golden colored oil with a nutty flavor. It is always used in small quantities, and added mostly towards the end of the cooking time. It is not the same as the sesame oil sold in natural food stores and should not be used to fry food.

SESAME SEEDS: there are two types, black and white; we used the white variety in this book. They are almost always toasted. To toast sesame seeds, stir over heat in a heavy skillet or spread on baking sheet and bake in 350°F oven about 5 minutes, the natural oil will brown the seeds.

SHRIMP: most of these recipes use fresh uncooked shrimp; shell and devein before use.

SNOW PEAS: also known as Chinese pea pods.

SPINACH: prepared by removing stems, cook leaves as recipes indicate.

EGG ROLL SKINS: are sold frozen in several different sizes; thaw before using; keep covered with a damp cloth until ready to use.

SQUID: is a type of mollusc; also known as calamari. Buy cleaned squid to make preparation easier.

SUGAR

Dark Brown Sugar: a soft fine granulated sugar with molasses present which gives it its characteristic color.

Superfine Sugar: fine granulated table sugar.

Sugar: we used a coarse granulated table sugar.

TOMATO PASTE: a concentrated tomato puree used as a flavoring.

VERMICELLI: we used rice vermicelli, also known as rice noodles.

VINEGAR: we used both white and brown (malt) vinegar.

WATERMELON: large green skinned melon with crisp juicy red flesh.

WATER CHESTNUTS: small white crisp bulbs with a brown skin. Canned water chestnuts are peeled and will keep for about a month, covered, in refrigerator.

WINE: we used good quality dry red and white wines.

Green Ginger: is an Australian-made alcoholic sweet wine infused with finely ground gingerroot.

WOK: is a Chinese cooking pan shaped like a large bowl with a rounded base. Flat-based woks are available for electric hotplates. To season a new wok before cooking, wash well with hot water and liquid detergent to remove any grease, wipe dry. Place wok over heat, add 3 tablespoons oil, 4 chopped green onions and 1 clove minced garlic. Swirl mixture over entire surface of wok, place over medium heat 5 minutes. Discard mixture, rinse pan under warm water, wipe dry. Do not scrub wok with any abrasive. Always wash in warm water, then wipe dry; this will protect the wok from rusting. Wipe over inside of wok with lightly oiled cloth, cover with plastic wrap to prevent dust settling on the surface during storage. Always heat wok before adding oil, then heat the oil before adding food to prevent food from sticking.

WONTON SKINS: are thin squares or rounds of fresh noodle dough, pale yellow in color. They are sold fresh or frozen; cover with a damp cloth to prevent drying out while using.

INDEX

CUP AND SPOON MEASUREMENTS

To ensure accuracy in your recipes use standard measuring equipment.

a) 8 fluid oz cup for measuring liquids.

b) a graduated set of four cups – measuring 1 cup, half, third and quarter cup – for items such as flour, sugar etc.
When measuring in these fractional cups level off at the brim.

c) a graduated set of five spoons: tablespoon (½ fluid oz liquid capacity), teaspoon, half, quarter amd eighth teaspoons.
All spoon measurements are level.

We have used large eggs with an average weight of 2oz each in all our recipes.